INTERNAL EVALUATION

Applied Social Research Methods Series
Volume 24

INTERNAL EVALUATION

Building Organizations from Within

Arnold J. Love

Applied Social Research Methods Series
Volume 24

SAGE Publications
International Educational and Professional Publisher
Newbury Park   London   New Delhi

For information address:

 SAGE Publications, Inc.
2455 Teller Road
Newbury Park, California 91320
E-mail: order@sagepub.com

SAGE Publications Ltd.
6 Bonhill Street
London EC2A 4PU
United Kingdom

SAGE Publications India Pvt. Ltd.
M-32 Market
Greater Kailash I
New Delhi 110 048 India

Printed in the United States of America

Library of Congress Cataloging-in-Publication Data

Love, Arnold J.
    Internal evaluation: building organizations from within / Arnold
J. Love.
        p.   cm. — (Applied social research methods)
    Includes bibliographical references and index.
    ISBN 0-8039-3200-6. — ISBN 0-8039-3201-4 (pbk.)
    1. Evaluation research (Social action programs) 2. Organizational
effectiveness—Evaluation. I. Title. II. Series: Applied social
research methods series.
    H62.L793   1991
    658.4'032—dc20   90-26167
                                                              CIP

97 98 99 00 01 02 03 13 12 11 10 9 8 7

Sage Production Editor: Michelle R. Starika

Contents

1

Internal Evaluation:
Scope and Challenge

Internal evaluation has been growing rapidly during the last few years. Disenchantment with external evaluators, funding cuts for large-scale evaluations, and widespread concern with the poor utilization of evaluations have spurred this growth. The radical shift from external to internal evaluations marks a major transition in the field of evaluation (House, 1986; Patton, 1982). The major impetus for the change came when internal evaluation began to be recognized as an indispensable tool for managers and an essential part of the management process (Love, 1983a; Sonnichsen & Schick, 1986). In the words of Attkisson and Broskowski (1978), "evaluation is primarily a process within on-going organizational management, decision making, and planning. . . . Program evaluation must be viewed as an integral aspect of organizational design and organizational development (p. 22)." Organizations in all sectors (private, public, and voluntary) now are embracing a flexible capacity for internal evaluation as fundamental to their management and ongoing improvement, as illustrated in these cases:

Case 1: The head of human resources for a *Fortune* 500 firm wants her internal evaluation staff to appraise the impact of a series of noontime fitness and life-style programs on job satisfaction and group morale.

Case 2: A government agency conducts regular internal evaluation studies to improve the performance of federally funded programs and maintain accountability for the use of public funds.

Case 3: The internal evaluation unit of a municipal school board studies the participation rates in a literacy program. The director of education needs this information to answer criticisms brought to the city council that the board is not responsive to the needs of minority groups and the disadvantaged.

Case 4: A manager in a community agency wants internal evaluators to find out if clients are benefiting from the services of the agency.

1

DEFINING INTERNAL EVALUATION

Internal evaluation is the process of using staff members who have the responsibility for evaluating programs or problems of direct relevance to an organization's managers. The key terms here are *internal, staff members, responsibility,* and *managers* (Clifford & Sherman, 1983). These characteristics help distinguish the internal evaluator from external consultants, academic researchers, and funding agency administrators or monitors in the following ways:

- As employees, internal evaluators are directly supervised by and report to persons who are part of the internal management of the organization. Usually internal evaluators are independent of the program they are evaluating, but, nonetheless they are part of the overall organization. In contrast, external evaluators are independent of both the program and the organization they are evaluating.
- Internal evaluators and managers have the ongoing responsibility for evaluation in the organization. With external evaluators, however, the primary responsibility for evaluation may rest with a funding body, a legislative committee, or a group of stockholders.
- The foci of internal evaluators' efforts are the concerns of the managers of the organization. In contrast, external evaluators usually study issues of interest to persons outside the organization being evaluated (e.g., funders, policymakers).

THE PLAN OF THIS BOOK

This book intends to reach several audiences: students of evaluation, internal evaluation professionals, managers, and the consumers of internal evaluation information, such as stockholders and funders. In North America, internal evaluations now account for an estimated three quarters of all evaluation activities. Yet little is known about how to harness the value of internal evaluation and avoid its pitfalls. The first purpose of this book is to present a coherent theory of internal evaluation that shows how internal evaluation fits with other aspects of organizational life (Chapter 2). The second purpose is to delineate the essential steps of the internal evaluation process (Chapter 3) and to describe the major internal evaluation methods (Chapters 4 through 8). For students and new internal evaluators, the exercises at the end of each section will afford them the opportunity to practice the concepts and skills of internal evaluation in real-world settings. The third major reason for writing this book is to expose internal evaluators and senior managers to a broad spectrum of useful internal evaluation methods, thereby helping them to expand their horizons and take full advantage of the power of internal evaluation. With this in mind, the book presents the stages of internal evaluation growth (Chapter 2), ways of identifying users' needs and selecting appropriate evaluation methods (Chapter 3), and the evaluation techniques associated with each stage (Chapters 4 through 8). Discussions about techniques emphasize the vantage points and practical concerns of internal evaluators, making the book a valuable desktop reference for internal evaluation practitioners.

COMPARISONS TO OTHER TYPES OF RESEARCH ACTIVITIES

One way of understanding internal evaluation is to contrast it to other types of research activities. Although internal evaluation depends heavily on the methods and models of behavioral science as used here, it is not rooted exclusively in that tradition. For example, internal evaluation draws upon a wide variety of techniques from systems, information, and management sciences.

Internal evaluation differs considerably from other approaches in its goals, assumptions, sponsors, and audiences, and in the relationship between the investigators and the other members of the organization. Internal evaluation is a form of *action research* (Krech, 1946; Lewin, 1948) that supports *organizational development* and *planned change* (Huse & Cummings, 1985). Consequently those responsible for internal evaluations often are responsible not only for analyzing problems and offering recommendations, but also for correcting difficulties and implementing solutions (Sonnichsen, 1988).

Unlike *nonapplied, academic research,* the focus of internal evaluation is usually a specific topic of immediate concern to managers. Internal evaluation is a powerful organizational intervention, as well as an investigative method. The study methodology is tailored to the constraints posed by political and practical considerations.

Internal evaluation is closer to *evaluation research* (Rossi & Freeman, 1982, p. 20), which is the use of social research methods to improve the planning, monitoring, and assessing the costs and out-comes of human service programs. Internal evaluation differs from evaluation research in the types of questions it addresses (Smith, 1987). Internal evaluation questions concentrate on management and policy issues, rather than on evaluative research questions alone. Also, internal evaluation is used for more than evaluating social programs. Private businesses, governmental agencies, comptrollers, and accrediting bodies, among others, use internal evaluation methods successfully.

Instead of focusing primarily on the outcomes of a program for its participants, internal evaluation defines effectiveness more broadly to include factors such as equity, acceptability, and political rationality. Evaluation research tends to judge the process of program delivery in terms of whether the program was implemented according to plan. Internal evaluation is similar to *organizational assessment* (Lawler, Nadler, & Cammann, 1980) and *organizational diagnosis* (Harrison, 1987) in its focus on the broader program and factors that influence its performance, including its structure, operations, and management. Above all else, internal evaluation is a management activity in which managers and internal evaluators alike play crucial roles.

THE PROS AND CONS OF
INTERNAL EVALUATION

Potential Advantages of Internal Evaluation

By reason of being part of an organization, the internal evaluator has firsthand knowledge of the organization's philosophy, policies, procedures, products, personnel, and management. This permits the selection of evaluation methods tailored to the reality of the organization. The long-term commitment of the internal evaluator permits the formation of positive working relationships with management and staff. This goes far in reducing the normal anxiety associated with any form of evaluation or performance measures.

Many internal evaluators are generalists who are expert both in technical domains and in all aspects of the corporate operation. With this form of credibility, the internal evaluator is in an excellent position to communicate relevant and timely evaluation information to line managers and staff. It also enables the internal evaluator to participate in long-range planning exercises, making crucial evaluative information available for strategic planning and policy decisions (Adie

& Thomas, 1987). Moreover, by consulting and providing information to various levels within the organization, the internal evaluator can encourage the greater utilization of evaluation information. The benefits of internal evaluation extend beyond individuals and groups to the organization as an whole. Developing the internal evaluation resource is an investment. The contract evaluator may be hired for a specific assignment, but the internal evaluator or internal evaluation unit is an enduring corporate resource. As a corporate resource the internal evaluator can assist in obtaining the information required by senior managers, funding bodies, or higher echelons of government for their planning and accountability purposes, as well as meet the information needs of the organization itself.

Potential Disadvantages of Internal Evaluation

A manager may prefer external evaluators when specialized skills are required and persons with them are not practical to keep on staff, or when the perspective of an outside observer is necessary (Tripoldi, Fellin, & Epstein, 1971). When the purpose of the evaluation is accountability to outside parties (e.g., funders, legislators, shareholders), external evaluators carry greater credibility as objective evaluators than do internal evaluators. Although they function independently, internal evaluators often are seen as employees who are accountable to the organization's management and subject to all of the attendant pressures of organizational life (Kennedy, 1983). In fact both external and internal evaluators have their biases, and true objectivity is an elusive commodity. Chapter 3 offers strategies for increasing the dependability of internal evaluation data and for improving the credibility of internal evaluations.

EVALUATION AS A MANAGEMENT ACTIVITY: UNDERSTANDING THE ROLES OF MANAGERS AND INTERNAL EVALUATORS

A constant theme of this book is that effective internal evaluation provides an indispensable support for managers. What seems to be an ideal marriage between managers and evaluators, however, has been marked by tension, misunderstanding, and conflicting values and intentions (Neigher & Metlay, 1983). The first step in developing effective internal evaluation, therefore, is forging a common mission and positive relationship between managers and evaluators. To do this, one must be clear about the roles of evaluators and managers.

What Is Management?

Management is both a process and a profession. It is a social and technical process of coordinating scarce human, physical, and information resources to achieve intended results. A basic tenet of management theory is that the process of management is basically the same whether the organization is a major multinational corporation, a highly centralized government department, or a nonprofit organization. This belief is predicated on the assumption that management is a universal process that embodies general principles. The functions assumed by managers, taken together, constitute the management process.

The general principles of management were introduced by Henri Fayol in the 1920s. Fayol was a mining engineer and the chief executive officer of a French company. He was one of the first to define management principles from the perspective of a practicing manager. In his book *General and Industrial Management* (Fayol, 1929), he defined management in terms of what managers do: leading, planning, organizing, controlling, and coordinating.

On the surface the idealized view of the rational manager seems highly compatible with the idealized view of the internal evaluator as technical analyst. The conflict between managers and evaluators, however, has been well-known for a long time (Attkisson & Broskowski, 1978; Guba, 1969; Neigher & Metlay, 1983; Weiss, 1973). Although this conflict may surprise some people, unfortunately, friction between managers and evaluators is the rule rather than the exception. To understand this apparent contradiction better, let us examine the worldviews of managers and evaluators.

Managers' Stereotypes of Evaluators

The manager sees the evaluator as naive and impractical, in terms of both the realities of organizational life and the methods used for evaluations. The manager's complex web of internal and external contacts provides a continuous flow of timely soft information about the real world, whereas the evaluator offers academic esoterica. The manager must make rapid decisions and act, whereas the evaluator pursues convoluted methodologies and reflects on the findings in the light of innumerable study limitations. The manager is a believer in people and programs, a partisan advocate and supporter; by contrast, the evaluator is a doubter who is uncommitted to anything or anyone. Finally, the manager is warm and outgoing, a leader and part of a team, as the evaluator sits in perpetual shade, cool and aloof, a lone wolf detached from the pack.

Evaluators' Stereotype of Managers

In comparison, the evaluator sees the manager as expedient, seeking quick fixes for problems and programs and minimizing the importance of ethical guidelines and research standards. The manager's reliance on informal contacts and soft data leads to decisions made on the basis of unreliable information. The impulsive action of managers in response to day-to-day pressures eschews enduring and creative long-term solutions. Rather than being a promoter of a pet program or service, the evaluator is committed to truth obtained after a fair and objective test. The evaluator does not sell a program or become enmeshed in the short-term goals of an organizational unit. Above all, the evaluator is a craftsman adhering to high professional standards and the long-term goals of the organization.

The Metaphorical Manager

As an applied field, management still continues to be defined by the work managers do. There is considerable disagreement, however, about the usefulness of Fayol's original functions, because a wide variety of a manager's tasks do not permit simple classification. Although each function seems equally important, there is growing awareness that the emphasis placed on each function changes greatly with the level of management and that the practice of management is affected by the organizational culture and changes in the external environment.

The complex and paradoxical nature of management has given rise to alternate methods of description. Metaphors are used to describe managers in terms of images. Perhaps the most popular metaphor is to compare the manager with an orchestra conductor. The metaphor shows how the manager integrates individual parts into a whole, just as an orchestra conductor creates beautiful music through the coordinated interaction of individual instruments and performers (Drucker, 1954; Neigher & Metlay, 1983).

Sayles (1964) offers a version of the same metaphor that is less idealized and captures some of the turbulence of the manager's world. In his view, the orchestra conductor struggles to maintain a melodious performance "while the orchestra members are having various personal difficulties, stage hands are moving music stands, alternating excessive heat and cold are creating audience and instrument problems, and the sponsor of the concert is insisting on irrational changes in the program" (p. 162).

What Do Managers Really Do?

Research by Mintzberg (1975, 1980) also challenges the orchestra-conductor metaphor and, along with it, the usefulness of defining the management process in terms of the traditional management functions. Mintzberg sought answers to the question, "What do managers *really* do?" He concluded that there were three main clusters of roles associated with the manager's job:

Exercising authority. The manager exercises direct authority by hiring, training, and supervising staff. This leadership role stems from the responsibility the manager has for the work of people in his or her organizational unit. The manager practices indirect authority through a variety of interpersonal roles that reflect the leadership of the manager, such as figurehead, motivator of staff to meet the organization's goals, liaison with persons inside and outside the organization, and protector of the unit's autonomy.

Processing information. Although the manager is usually identified with the leadership role, many of the manager's interpersonal activities, in fact, serve the information processing roles of the manager's job. Much of the manager's job involves receiving and transmitting information. The manager must supply information needed to subordinates in the unit who have no other access to it. As representative of the unit, the manager provides information about the unit's performance to a variety of audiences.

Making decisions. Information is crucial not for its own sake, but as a necessary resource for decision making. The ultimate performance of the organization stems from the cumulative quality of the decisions of its managers. Decisions are the means for achieving the organization's objectives. Managers are responsible for their decisions; their effectiveness is measured by the results of those decisions. This is true whether the managers are line managers or chief executive officers, or whether the organization is profit-making or nonprofit.

Table 1.1

Successful and Unsuccessful Roles of Internal Evaluators

Successful Roles	Unsuccessful Roles
• Management Consultant	• Spy
• Decision-Support Specialist	• Hatchet Man
• Management Information Specialist	• Dragon Lady
• Systems Generalist	• Number Cruncher
• Expert Troubleshooter	• Organizational Conscience
• Advocate	• Organizational Memory
• Systematic Planner	

SUCCESSFUL AND UNSUCCESSFUL ROLES OF INTERNAL EVALUATORS

Once we understand what managers really do, then it is clear that the differences between managers and evaluators are *not* true personality traits, but rather differences in backgrounds, roles, goals, values, and frames of reference (Clifford & Sherman, 1983; Neigher & Metlay, 1983). We have seen that there are many common elements between the two professions, but there are also significant differences. We have seen that appreciating these perspectives of managers and internal evaluators builds mutual respect and a solid partnership reflecting their complementary roles.

These distinctions are important because they affect the evaluator's role and how he or she operates. They are at the root of the major problems in understanding between internal evaluators and managers. This is evident when successful and unsuccessful roles of internal evaluators are compared (see Table 1.1).

Unsuccessful Roles

- *Spy.* The evaluator is a spy for management who collects information about the job performance of individuals.
- *Hatchet Man/Dragon Lady.* The evaluator collects data to support a foregone conclusion: the program, product, or service is not meeting expectations and it will be cut. The evaluator does the dirty work for senior managers. The evaluation is a ruse for collecting data to administer a coup de grace to a manager or program.

- *Number Cruncher.* The evaluator remains an isolated and aloof technician speaking in strange tongues about incomprehensible statistical topics. The evaluator does not have any rapport or empathy with the real-world pressures placed on managers and staff. By relying strongly on data from information systems that are likely to be inaccurate ("garbage in, garbage out"), the evaluator misses the forest for the trees and draws incorrect inferences from the data. The evaluator provides little information of use for decision making.
- *Organizational Conscience.* The evaluator undertakes evaluation studies for the purpose of accountability to external funders or administrative bodies. The studies employ rigorous measures of program effects using experimental designs and maintaining strict control over program activities. Because such control and experimental designs are virtually impossible to execute within the average organizational setting, results tend to be negative, creating a political and organizational trap for the evaluator.
- *Organizational Memory.* The evaluator has the responsibility of managing an information system containing archived data. The evaluator collects these data regularly and processes them at considerable expenditure of time and energy. Rarely do managers use this information for reporting or decision making: It just exists as part of an organizational memory. The evaluator is relegated to the role of clerk.

Successful Roles

- *Management Consultant.* The internal evaluator consults with managers on the use of data-based approaches to solving managerial problems. In this role, the evaluator is an organizational change agent, and the internal evaluator exercises his or her considerable organizational development and interpersonal skills.
- *Decision-Support Specialist.* The internal evaluator assists managers in their functions of planning and controlling and in their decision-making roles. This demonstrates the evaluator's technical and analytic skills and interpersonal and organizational skills.
- *Management Information Specialist.* The internal evaluator supports managers by providing information through paper and automated information systems. The internal evaluator is an expert at analyzing the manager's information needs, designing systems, ensuring data integrity, and providing information in a way that is useful to managers.
- *Systems Generalist.* The internal evaluator masters the organization's administrative systems and all aspects of the corporate operation. The evaluator also has special expertise in systems analysis.
- *Expert Troubleshooter.* The internal evaluator possesses formal training in management (or a related area) and firsthand experience in managing several areas of the organization. The evaluator has exemplary skills in

organizational diagnosis and problem solving. The evaluator's managerial and technical background, together with a reputation for integrity and access to senior managers, lend the credibility needed to diagnose problems and recommend solutions. The troubleshooter may manage the implementation of the solution.

• *Advocate.* The internal evaluator is a change agent who influences managers to use information to become active problem solvers. Internal evaluators and their supervisors are active participants in the organizational process of making decisions and implementing recommendations that lead to program improvements (Sonnichsen, 1987, 1988). This is a recent role for internal evaluators, and it should not be confused with the negative roles associated with the Advocacy-Adversary model (Patton, 1982) and the Advocacy model (Windle, 1979; Windle & Neigher, 1978). In these two models, evaluators become biased "champions" for the program, assisting the program by emphasizing its strong points and/or helping it in its competition for funding.

• *Systematic Planner.* The internal evaluator expedites planning by encouraging policies and designing procedures for establishing a periodic planning process, and by systematically collecting the information needed for planning. The evaluator facilitates the interpersonal process of planning. The evaluator analyzes and synthesizes diverse data about the organization's internal and external environment to develop alternative futures for deliberation by management.

NEW ROLES FOR INTERNAL EVALUATORS

Question: Who is an external consultant?
Answer: Someone to whom management pays exorbitant fees to do what management is supposed to do for itself.

Robert McHugh (1986, p. 46) used this provocative definition to make the point that internal staff have opportunities to become consultants to management and the board of directors. If they won't, an external consultant will be used to fill the gap. Internal evaluators share in these opportunities because evaluation is a integral part, in some way or another, of all areas of an organization's operations. If internal evaluators can assume the role of evaluation specialists and provide opportunities for the organization to improve its performance, then they have the right, if not the obligation, to assume a consulting role addressing a broad spectrum of the organization's problems. As internal management consultants, the five major functions of the internal evaluator are supporting, diagnosing, consulting, informing, and linking.

Supporting. Supporting involves assisting the manager in the exercise of authority by providing information clarifying the organization's mission, purpose, goals, and objectives; describing programs and services accurately; describing efforts and the achievement of results accurately; identifying factors leading to a more effective and efficient use of human and physical resources; maintaining the quality of products or services; and specifying factors contributing to higher work satisfaction and productivity.

Diagnosing. Diagnosing means identifying, verifying, and clearly articulating problems; determining how critical the problems are by measuring the gap between goals and performance; collecting relevant internal and external information to help the manager develop alternative scenarios; assessing the risk associated with alternative scenarios; weighing the costs and benefits of alternatives; and assisting in developing procedures for implementing and monitoring the implementation of the solution.

Consulting. Consulting means providing meaningful information to managers and their staff in a way that fosters a data-based problem-solving process, encourages creativity, develops the ability to use the information, and facilitates action. The internal evaluator coaches managers about how to use information for analyzing and organizing work effectively and for achieving the goals and objectives of the unit and the organization.

Informing. Informing means communicating information in a timely and understandable manner to managers about the performance of their plans and the success of their efforts to correct deviations in those plans.

Linking. Linking means using information to identify and solve problems that have implications in other parts of the organization or in the organization's external environment. Linking involves adopting a strategic systems approach that recognizes the organization's long-term goals as important. The linking process uses information to nurture collaborative relationships, joint problem solving, and resource sharing throughout the organization and with the external environment.

BUILDING THE PARTNERSHIP BETWEEN
MANAGERS AND INTERNAL EVALUATORS

Effective internal evaluation requires a radical change in the traditional way evaluators and managers think, feel, and behave toward their organizations (Wildavsky, 1972). Because internal evaluation is an integral part of the management of the organization, the internal evaluator has a responsibility to support managers. The internal evaluator has a commitment to improving the organization through supporting managers directly in their roles of exercising authority, processing information, and making decisions. This is done by observing the principles of complementary roles, supporting managers, and realism.

Complementary Roles

The roles of the internal evaluator are clearly complementary to those of managers. Managers have the organizational responsibility for evaluation. Managers and internal evaluators have the joint responsibility to determine what data are required to meet the manager's information needs. The evaluator, however, has the primary responsibility for assessing information needs, determining the feasibility of answering those needs with existing information, and designing alternative strategies. The evaluator must appraise the timeliness, value, and cost of collecting evaluative information. The evaluator must ascertain what analyses must be performed and the best format for presenting results. The manager must consider the conclusions suggested by the data and then decide on the course of action. Finally, the manager must weigh the political and organizational implications of implementing proposed changes.

Supporting Managers

Recognizing evaluation as a management activity reflects a positive attitude toward managers. Internal evaluators acknowledge that managers want to be accountable and seek evaluative information to assess needs, plan program activities, improve programs, and in general make better decisions. Through their understanding of organizational behavior, internal evaluators know that managers must reduce uncertainty or risk involved in making a decision. They know that managers want to define issues or problems that are management decision dilemmas. They realize that managers want to make authoritative decisions concerning potential responses to problems. In particular, internal evaluators appreciate that managers, facing the ever-changing political and economic environments, want to make better decisions about organizational and program options and the use of scarce resources.

Realism

A positive attitude toward managers does not imply naïveté. Many managers have value systems that scoff at the serious use of evaluative information (Carter, 1983, 1987). These managers "know" that a clear description of client needs, program activities, and program outcomes creates less room for maneuvering during budget negotiations. They "know" that it's easier to obscure what is delivered than to clarify what is expected. They "know" that funders, politicians, and the public are more impressed by passionate testimonials than by a balanced report. Internal evaluators must demonstrate to these managers, quietly and persistently, that they are cheating themselves and robbing themselves of success by ignoring the real potential of internal evaluation information. To do this, internal evaluators must prove their ability to improve the managers' performance by exercising positive roles.

SUMMARY

This chapter defines internal evaluation and illustrates its use in several types of organizations. It has compared internal evaluation with other types of research activities and has emphasized that internal evaluation is a management activity.

Effective internal evaluation requires forging a common mission and positive relationship between managers and evaluators. Understanding the roles of managers and evaluators is critical to this process. The manager's job centers around three clusters of roles: exercising authority, processing information, and making decisions. As an internal management consultant, the internal evaluator has five complementary sets of functions: supporting, diagnosing, consulting, informing, and linking. Internal evaluators must nurture positive roles (e.g., decision-support specialist, expert troubleshooter) and avoid negative ones (e.g., hatchet man/dragon lady, number cruncher). Effective internal evaluation requires a radical change in the traditional way evaluators and managers think, feel, and behave toward their organizations. For their part, evaluators must forge strong bonds with managers by recognizing that their roles are complementary to those of managers and by developing a keen appreciation of the manager's job. Being realistic, internal evaluators know they must demonstrate the potential of internal evaluation to improve managers' performance by exercising positive roles.

PREPARING FOR EXERCISES

Because internal evaluation takes place in an organizational context, many of the exercises that follow will be more meaningful if you are able to interview a manager and staff in a real program or organization to complete your assignments. You may use an organization where you currently work or one where you have access to persons and information. Usually your course instructor will have list of organizations that are willing to accept placements, and the name of a contact person. These placement locations range from private businesses to community agencies to campus organizations. Although some may have an internal evaluator on staff or an internal evaluation unit, this is not necessary for the assignments.

A form letter of introduction from your instructor describing the purpose of the course is usually sufficient to gain the necessary cooperation. The letter should describe the purpose of the course (e.g., to learn how internal evaluators can help managers solve problems and improve their programs). If the assignments are a course requirement, then the letter should mention that fact. The letter should stress that as little of the manager's and staff's time will be taken as possible—usually less than three or four hours spread over the period of the course. The letter should inform the manager that a real evaluation will not take place, and that all written reports are confidential. Only the course instructor will read them.

The next step is to have an interview with the contact person to clarify the nature of your assignments. If the contact person has any additional questions about the placement, have the contact person speak with your instructor.

Because many organizations are interested in internal evaluation, usually you will experience little difficulty in finding a suitable placement and obtaining the desired cooperation from managers and staff.

EXERCISES

1. Briefly explain how these factors serve to distinguish internal evaluators from external evaluators: (a) purpose of evaluations; (b) users of the evaluation; (c) evaluation approach; (d) relationship with the organization; (e) length of involvement; and (f) commitment to the organization.

2. Name at least two characteristics that distinguish internal evaluation from (a) academic research and (b) evaluation research.

3. Ted and Alice are planning to lose weight and trim their thighs in time for the swimsuit season. In their search for a suitable weight loss program, they are deluged with claims about the "miracles" accomplished by participants in each of the competing programs. What recommendations would you give our dynamic duo about the pros and cons of accepting data from internal evaluations conducted by the weight loss programs in helping them make this decision?

4. Observe a manager in your organization for a morning or an afternoon. Then describe his or her roles (a) according to the traditional functions of managers, and (b) following the decision-making model. In your opinion which fits better? How well does the orchestra-conductor metaphor fit your manager? What implications does this have for an internal evaluator in this organization?

5. If your organization has an internal evaluation function, interview a manager and an internal evaluator. In what areas are their viewpoints and roles in conflict? What roles of the internal evaluator do they see as successful and unsuccessful ones? What strategies can you suggest for bridging the gap and developing a partnership between the two?

2

The Organizational Context of Internal Evaluation

Chapter 1 introduced the idea that internal evaluation is a function that takes place within an organizational context. The organizational context strongly influences both the choice of evaluation methods and the use of evaluation results (Love, 1983b). A deeper understanding of the organizational aspects of internal evaluation systems is essential for anyone who is concerned with the intelligent management of organizational change and improvement (Hopwood, 1974). Once the organizational aspects of internal evaluation systems are recognized, strategies that enhance the effectiveness of internal evaluation can be examined and implemented. The aim of this chapter is to present a body of theory that provides a useful conceptual structure for understanding and practicing internal evaluation in the dynamic context of the modern organization.

Given that it is beyond the scope of this book to address the entire body of management theory, this chapter begins with a review of the theories that are essential for the practice of internal evaluation. Next, attention turns to the crucial role of information in managing an organization, a point first introduced when discussing managers' roles in Chapter 1. Then the chapter describes how organizations make decisions under conditions of uncertainty. This provides the rationale for using internal evaluation as a tool for increasing an organization's ability to process information, and for increasing the effectiveness of organizational decision making. Described next are the major steps in the decision-making process and how internal evaluation can assist with each step. Then the focus moves to defining managers' information requirements at each management level, including a close examination of the major attributes of managers' information needs. The chapter then concludes with descriptions of a developmental model of the growth of internal evaluation capability.

ESSENTIAL THEORIES OF
ORGANIZATIONAL MANAGEMENT

The Economic Theory of the Organization

The economic theory of the organization identifies the chief role of the manager of a profit-making firm as that of maximizing the net present value of stockholder wealth. The criterion of economic rationality, in turn, calls for managers to make the best (or optimal) decisions for their organizations (Becker, 1977). In nonprofit organizations, the manager is also expected to behave in a precise and rational way to maximize the utility of public expenditures. This viewpoint assumes that there is a standard procedure for making decisions that can lead to a proven best solution. It also assumes that the state of the art in rational decision making can be defined purely in mathematical terms.

The Behavioral Theory of the Organization

Herbert Simon (1961) and Richard Cyert and James March (1963) challenged the normative economic view and proposed a behavioral theory of the organization in its place. They adopted a *systems approach* that viewed the organization as a whole, composed of interrelated subsystems, and decision-making behavior as the means for achieving results and solving problems. Thus the organizational structure provides the framework for decision-making behavior. The quality and the process of decision making, in turn, are shaped by the nature of the organizational structure. The theory describes decision-making behavior in a climate of uncertainty filled with contradictory goals, tenuous outcomes, and vague information. The behavioral theory of the organization applies to profit-making and nonprofit organizations alike.

Cyert and March saw the multiple and conflicting goals of organizations as a natural result of a negotiation process among coalitions of individuals with a vested interest in the organization. The bargaining among these multiple constituencies involves concessions called *side payments* (e.g., salaries, rank, and preferential working conditions), which are used to balance the demands of competing interest groups. The net result of these negotiations is a compromise set of goals. The more unstable the coalitions, the more likely that the goals will be vague and conflicting.

Once these agreements are made, they are preserved by *mutual control systems*. For example, the organizational structure allocates authority and responsibility, thereby limiting the influence of different coalitions. The annual budget serves as a guarantee by senior management to provide a level of support that permits the various departmental coalitions to exist. Policies, procedures, regulations, and professional standards also exert a self-confining control on the interest groups.

THE CENTRAL ROLE OF INFORMATION IN ORGANIZATIONS

The Information Function

Nobel laureate Herbert Simon (1960) considered managing to be synonymous with the process of decision making. In Chapter 1 it was noted that the manager's job involves not only making decisions, but also seeing that the organization makes decisions effectively. To coordinate their activities in response to external and internal changes, managers must receive, process, and act on information effectively. Jay Galbraith (1977) argues that the way an organization processes information is at its core and that it determines the design of an organization's structure.

Evaluating is a key information-processing and decision-making function of managers. In the ever-changing environments of modern organizations, managers must take into account the effect of each individual decision on the entire system. Given that the organization's subsystems and processes are interrelated, a decision in one area might have an unintended impact on another part of the organization. The options available and the potential effects of a decision, therefore, must be evaluated *before* implementation. In turn, evaluation feedback provides information about the effects of current decisions *after* implementation that helps guide future decision making. In the turbulent organizational environment, the situation constantly changes, making decision making and internal evaluation a continuous and dynamic process.

Programmed and Nonprogrammed Decisions

Herbert Simon (1960) described a continuum of decisions with programmed and nonprogrammed decisions at opposite ends. In this context programmed means a specific set of rules or procedures that guides the responses of the organization. Programmed decisions are routine decisions that have a definite procedure. Programmed decisions focus on short-term control. Examples of programmed decisions are using evaluation information for scheduling appointments, or for determining when a new supply of widgets should be ordered. Much of the job of frontline and middle managers involves developing methods for resolving programmed decisions effectively and efficiently.

In contrast, nonprogrammed decisions are novel and unstructured. They must be made when a problem is new, complex, difficult to grasp, or requires a unique solution. Senior managers should be concerned primarily with nonprogrammed decisions. Long-range planning and strategy making demand nonprogrammed decisions. For example, planning the first Apollo space flight required nonprogrammed decisions involving complex intelligence, design, and evaluation activities. Other examples of nonprogrammed decisions are using evaluation information to help design a new advertising campaign, change a government regulatory system, or modify university entrance criteria.

DECISION MAKING UNDER
CONDITIONS OF UNCERTAINTY

Given the inherent productivity payoffs attached to programmed decisions, a major responsibility of managers is identifying decisions that can be programmed, and then programming them. It is estimated that up to 80% of the decisions in a well-managed organization could be programmed. Organizations in stable and predictable environments can benefit from programmed decisions by instituting rules and procedures to coordinate activities. The problem is that organizations in complex and turbulent environments, however, cannot rely on rules, procedures, and other traditional methods of information processing.

In these organizations, decisions must be made immediately in the face of unexpected changes. This situation increases the flow of information to the point where the capacity of the managers and the organization to process information is overloaded. An organization is in serious trouble when the efforts of senior managers are constantly diverted to solving operational decisions (Grandori, 1984). Unfortunately, this is the situation that frequently develops when decision making occurs under conditions of uncertainty.

As the demand for information increases, therefore, so does the need for flexible and adaptable organizational designs (Galbraith, 1982). Creating suitable organizational structures is called the *process* function of managers. The two general responses to the problem of information overload are (a) reducing the need for information, and (b) increasing the capacity to process information.

Reducing the Need for Information

Reducing the organization's need for information can be achieved by two strategies: creating slack resources, or creating self-contained units or departments (Galbraith, 1973; Joyce, 1986).

Creating slack resources. The manager cannot cope with conflicting goals and the diverse values of interest groups in a rational manner. Because managers operate under conditions of uncertainty, they compensate for the margin of error in their estimates by obtaining discretionary funds, material, and personnel in excess of their immediate needs. Cyert and March (1963) called these excess side payments *organizational slack.* Although it may be perceived as wasteful in a predictable environment, sufficient slack is essential for organizational survival and to provide for future growth.

Creating self-contained units. As an organization grows, it may be divided into smaller organizational units through a hierarchical organizational structure. Through this mechanism, the apparent size of the organization is kept small, and managers can continue to make use of programmed decisions. A system for setting goals and measuring their achievement is usually required, however, to coordinate the efforts of individual units with those of the organization as a whole.

In conditions of uncertainty, the manager makes decisions by addressing a few goals at a time and using organizational slack to glue the seams together. With experience, managers tend to adopt a set of simple rules and procedures for resolving problems that affect the performance of their tasks. Organizations with many different programs, professional groups, and consumers or clients attempt to reduce uncertainty by *decentralizing decisions* so that a simple set of rules can be applied to a limited number of situations. These organizations are known as *loosely coupled* because they have a loose gathering of groups of persons that join together for specific purposes.

Example: In a mental health clinic a psychiatrist, a social worker, and a child care worker may become the treatment team for one client, and a social worker, a speech pathologist, and an occupational counselor may constitute the team for another client. This arrangement gives the organization greater flexibility and adaptability.

Increasing the Capacity to Process Information

In the face of information overload, another choice is to increase the organization's capacity to process information. This may be accomplished by investing in decision support systems and by creating boundary-spanning roles (Galbraith, 1973; Tushman & Scanlan, 1981).

Investing in management support systems. Managers can cope with information overload by processing information more rapidly or by aggregating the data more efficiently. This may be achieved by using specialized management support staff, such as internal evaluators, and computerized information systems. The use of internal evaluation as a management support system is increasing rapidly. Two factors have aided this growth. First, training in evaluation has increased the supply of internal evaluators. Second, rapid advances in microcomputer hardware and software (coupled with sharp price decreases) have made powerful computer technology accessible to virtually every organization.

Creating boundary-spanning roles. Creating self-contained units differentiates functions and delegates decisions to the appropriate levels. At the same time, however, it creates the problem of coordinating information and integrating the decentralized departments. The strategy of creating boundary spanning roles facilitates making decisions that cross departmental boundaries, or that involve the external environment. Internal evaluators have boundary spanning roles both within and outside the organization. Within the organization, internal evaluators span boundaries by providing liaison, project leadership, and management consulting across departments. Outside the organization, internal evaluators obtain information that affects the organization's survival and growth, identifies new markets and sources of funding, enhances the status of the organization, and coordinates services among service providers.

THE PROCESS OF DECISION MAKING

Herbert Simon (1960) recognized the three principal phases to decision making: (a) finding situations requiring a decision, (b) finding possible courses of action, and (c) choosing among alternative courses of action. The first phase Simon called *intelligence activity,* the second phase *design activity,* and the third phase *choice activity.* To these we may add the steps of implementing the decision and measuring the results of the decision (see Figure 2.1). The important point is that decisions themselves are the end products of a decision-making process. In general, managers spend much of their time in the intelligence and design phases of the decision-making process, and comparatively little time actually making the choices. For problems that occur frequently, the entire sequence of steps is not needed. If guidelines (i.e., programmed decisions) can be created to resolve such problems, developing and evaluating alternative solutions are not required each time a problem of this kind appears. In contrast, nonprogrammed decisions require using the entire sequence. This demands more of the manager's time and effort because the risks associated with different alternatives in new and complex situations must be carefully assessed. Although methods exist for estimating the probable risk of each alternative, nonprogrammed decisions inevitably take vastly more time than programmed decisions (Hodder & Riggs, 1985).

The effective manager follows a process of decision making to generate programmed and nonprogrammed decisions. As a decision support system, effective internal evaluation assists the manager to make better decisions. Under conditions of uncertainty and risk, effective internal evaluation permits the manager to cope with the situation by reducing the volume of nonessential information and increasing the capacity to process information essential to decision making. In general, effective internal evaluation improves the quality of managers' decision making at every step in the process, whether it is identifying opportunities or problems, finding and exploring alternatives, evaluating alternatives, or evaluating the results of implementing the decision. Each of these steps will be discussed briefly and illustrated with an example drawn from the experiences of a municipal nursing home manager.

PHASE   PROCESS

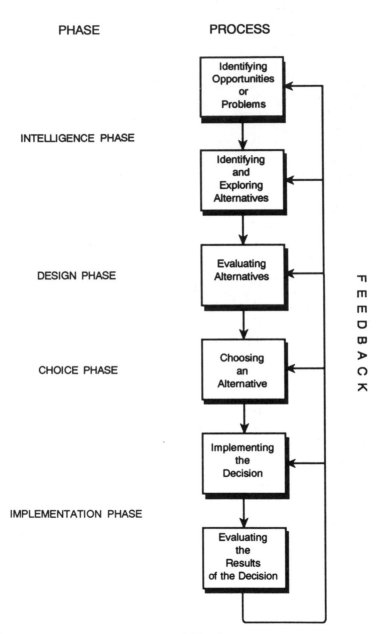

Figure 2.1. Phases in the Decision Making Process

Intelligence phase support. Internal evaluators can play a major role in the intelligence aspect of decision making. This involves gathering, analyzing, and synthesizing the information needed for strategic, policy, planning, and other nonprogrammed decisions. Internal evaluation can help a manager identify opportunities or problems by forecasting changes in the external environment, by determining whether policies were adequately established and how compliance with them can be measured, and by identifying gaps between goals and objectives and the required levels of achievement.

The importance of internal evaluation as a support for intelligence phase decision making often is overlooked. In the intelligence phase of decision making, internal evaluations facilitate bringing opportunities or problems to a manager's attention. A crucial role of managers at all levels is to be aware of situations requiring a decision. The role of internal evaluation is to help identify these situations; then the managers are responsible for assessing whether the situation requires a response. Internal evaluators have the important role of expanding the information environment to include external sources, thereby balancing the tendency of managers to rely too much on internal sources of information.

Example: Internal evaluation reports show that the occupancy rate for nursing homes set in municipal standards is being exceeded by over half of the homes. Projections show that the number of elderly will continue to rise, and the proposed housing stock will not meet the need. Clearly, this is a serious situation requiring the manager's attention.

Design phase support. In the design phase, internal evaluation can assist the manager in determining the feasibility of alternative courses of action. Internal evaluation can help by determining whether a genuine problem is being raised or only the symptom, and by searching the organization's internal and external environment for alternatives.

Example: Internal evaluators conduct a needs assessment study of elderly persons either currently in nursing homes or on the waiting lists. Using this information, internal evaluators work with the manager and a committee to explore alternate courses of action.

Choice phase support. In the choice phase, internal evaluation can help determine the consequences of each alternative. The manager uses evaluation criteria to determine the impact of alternative solutions. This impact can be measured several ways.

Example: The municipal manager and the committee measure the effects of mixing new nursing home beds, expanded homemaker services, and supported apartments. With this information and the costs for each alternative, the manager and committee negotiate the mix of housing and services that best satisfies the criteria.

Also, internal evaluation can assist the manager by investigating the range of potential alternatives and the probable consequences of each, by assessing the level of risk involved in the decision given the potential alternatives, and by determining whether other goals or objectives of the organization will be compromised if the alternative is chosen.

Example: The municipal manager works with internal evaluators to evaluate issues such as the quality of proposed alternate care, the accessibility of needed accommodations and services, and the risk of using less costly alternatives to nursing homes.

Implementation phase support. Finally, in the implementation phase, internal evaluation provides feedback. Internal evaluation also can help evaluate the results of the decision by measuring planned results against actual results and by judging the overall effectiveness of the decision.

Example: The municipal manager obtains an internal evaluation report monitoring actual utilization and costs of services, mortality rates, results of quality assurance reviews, and findings of client satisfaction interviews. The manager then compares the results with the initial plans. The manager reports the success of the decisions.

This example emphasized the use of both quantitative and qualitative methods in the nursing home decision process. In complex decisions and in situations of uncertainty, qualitative factors play a significant and complementary role in decision making. This point will be discussed in Chapter 3.

LEVELS OF DECISION MAKING

Types of decisions vary from one organizational level of decision making to another. Robert Anthony (1965, pp. 15-18), building on the work of Peter Drucker (1954), distinguished the purposes of decisions

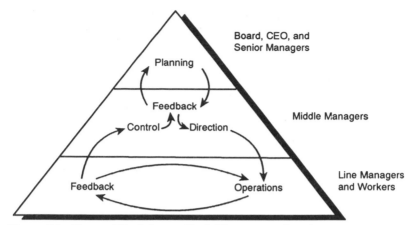

Figure 2.2. Types of Decisions at Each Management Level

made by each of the three levels of management. Simply stated, planning by senior managers determines what must be done, direction by middle managers defines how it is to be done, and operations by frontline managers do it. The feedback of what is done in operations is then evaluated and controlled. Information is continually recycled throughout the corporate structure.

Figure 2.2 illustrates this widely accepted scheme. Senior managers are responsible for strategic planning by deciding on organizational goals, changes in those goals, the resources used to attain the objectives, and on the policies regulating the acquisition, use, and disposal of those resources. Strategic decisions are long-term and set the overall direction of the total organization. Middle managers undertake management control by assuring that resources are obtained and used effectively and efficiently to accomplish the organization's goals. Management control decisions (also known as tactical decisions) are short-term and relate primarily to the use of resources. Frontline managers are responsible for operational control and ensure that specific tasks are carried out in keeping with their department's objectives.

As a key management decision support, an effective internal evaluation system must be responsive to the different information requirements at each of these management levels. Also, because the flow of information links one organizational level to another, the internal evaluator must be aware that the content and form of information about the same topic will change depending on who is using the information.

The 10 Major Attributes of
Information Needed by Managers

The first step in defining these different information needs is to examine the attributes of information required by managers for decision making at each organizational level (see Figure 2.3). The 10 major information attributes are:

(1) *Type of Questions.* Frontline managers want information that describes what is happening; that is, they want answers to "What is . . . ?" or "Who is . . . ?" types of questions. For example, a personnel manager may want to know, "What is the total and average salary for each department?" In contrast, senior managers want to know what will happen if an alternative solution is adopted, which is to say they want answers to "What if . . . ?" questions. For example, a senior manager may want to know, "What if my organization's overheads were to increase by 15% at the same time production increased by 10% or by 20%?"

(2) *Time Horizon.* Senior managers involved in strategic planning emphasize what is expected to happen in the future. Depending on the nature of the organization, the strategic management function has a broad time horizon stretching from 1 to 25 years. At the other extreme, operational managers want to know what is happening now. Middle managers are somewhere in between: They need to compare information about current operations with longitudinal data about past operations and horizontal data (i.e., current data from other departments) to detect and correct potential problems. The time horizon for middle managers usually extends from one month to five years.

(3) *Information Sources.* Each level of management needs data from different sources to make decisions. For operational control, data from *internal* sources are needed, such as the number of clients served or products sold. Higher level managers need more data from *external* sources, such as marketing information, and less from internal sources in making decisions.

(4) *Measurement.* Operational and managerial control demand *quantitative* data, whereas strategic planning and other nonprogrammed decisions place greater reliance on *qualitative* information, such as the qualitative evaluation of services and products. Informed opinion, intuition, insight, vision, and synthesis are used to balance facts and analysis.

(5) *Level of Detail.* Managers responsible for operational control want detailed information, even details about individual persons or events. For example, managers may want to know not only how many items were sold by each sales representative, but the types of items, their cost, and their profit margins. They may want to know the name of the top performer in the division. Middle managers want less detail and more

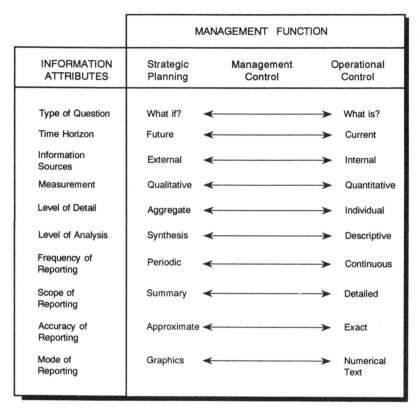

Figure 2.3. Attributes of Information Needed for Decision Making at Each Management Level

aggregate data for management control decisions. They are concerned with information about the performance of organizational units such as programs, departments, or divisions. Senior managers want information about the performance of the entire organization, and data must be highly aggregated. Internal evaluators assist this process by defining the basic data building blocks and then aggregating them for the desired management level.

(6) *Level of Analysis.* Operational control requires *descriptive* information in terms that help the manager guide the program or process being controlled. Middle managers need an *analysis* of the detailed descriptive information in order to identify patterns. For strategic planning, a *synthesis* of data that includes policy and long-term implications is essential.

(7) *Frequency of Reporting*. Line managers want continuous reporting because they need to monitor all aspects of operations. Middle and senior managers, in comparison, usually require information on a periodic basis (e.g., monthly or quarterly).

(8) *Scope of Reporting*. Operational managers want extensive and unabridged quantitative information, such as the current pupil-teacher ratio for each class or the number of vacant hospital beds. Likewise, they find detailed qualitative information important, such as case histories, verbatim interview data, or firsthand observational data. Rather than detail, middle managers need to identify variations from expected results. They want *exception reporting* so they can spot opportunities and problems quickly and initiate the needed action. Senior managers use exception reporting, together with highly summarized information and staff briefings, to identify critical questions and spot emerging trends.

(9) *Accuracy of Reporting*. Some management levels have a need for more accurate information than do others. Accurate information is expensive, and it is not needed in all circumstances. A projection of the sales of personal computers in the year 2025 does not require the same level of accuracy as does a report about the failure rate of a batch of computer microchips or the number of students enrolled in a course. Usually line and middle managers with control responsibility require more accuracy than top managers responsible for overall planning.

(10) *Mode of Reporting*. Operational managers are more likely to need reports that present numerical and text data. Middle managers require less detailed numerical and text data and need reports presenting plots or graphs to help isolate exceptions. At the strategic planning level, written reporting becomes less important, and greater emphasis is placed on presentations and briefings reporting information graphically.

DEVELOPING INTERNAL EVALUATION CAPABILITY

Internal evaluation capability tends to grow in stages. The developmental theory of internal evaluation describes the stages through which organizations generally proceed as they develop a progressively greater capacity for self-evaluation. Cliff Attkisson and Bill Hargreaves (1977) were among the first to identify stages of internal evaluation activities ordered on a developmental continuum. They noted that internal evaluation capability at a specific stage depends, at least partially, upon adequate capability at the previous stages. The general parameters of these stages are congruent with those identified in numerous empirical

TYPE OF EVALUATION INFORMATION MANAGEMENT	Inconsistent	Individual Managers Accountable	Formal Planning and Control	Standardized Definitions and Measurement	Shared Data Across Functions	Evaluation Information Resource Management
FOCUS	Individual Projects	Operational Level	Management Control Level	Management Control Level	Management Control Level	Strategic Planning Level
PRIMARY USERS	Scattered	Front-Line Managers	Middle Managers	Middle Managers and Senior Managers	Middle Managers and Senior Managers	Senior Managers
	Stage 1 Ad Hoc	Stage 2 Systematic	Stage 3 Goal	Stage 4 Effectiveness	Stage 5 Efficiency	Stage 6 Strategic Benefit

Figure 2.4. Developmental Stages of Internal Evaluation Capability

studies (Glaser & Kirkhart, 1982; Kirkhart, 1979; Kirkhart & Morgan, 1986; McCollough, 1975). Figure 2.4 shows the differences in primary users, focus, and evaluation information management at each developmental stage.

Stage 1: Ad Hoc Evaluation

The first stage of evaluation is called ad hoc evaluation. At this stage, managers recognize evaluation as a valuable tool to support their decision making, but it is used in an isolated fashion to provide information to individual managers or project teams on an ad hoc basis. Neither the organizational structure nor the evaluation process support a more systematic use of internal evaluation.

At the ad hoc stage, data are fragmented and largely subjective. Definitions of data and data collection methods are not standardized. Data about organizational and program inputs (e.g., financial and staff resources, demands for services, client needs) are not available routinely. Organizational and program goals and assumptions have not been made explicit, and the criteria for appraising quality or effectiveness are murky. The evaluation capability is primitive and inefficient. For example, there is no guarantee that useful data will be available when the manager needs them for decision making, and "one-shot" data procedures may have to be hurriedly implemented.

Stage 2: Systematic Internal Evaluation

At the systematic evaluation stage, the power of internal evaluation is focused at the operational level. Internal evaluation information is primarily descriptive ("What is?"). Generally both users and internal evaluation staff are held accountable for the development of systematic evaluation. The system is well documented and is designed using a modular approach that makes it easy to maintain and modify. Some organizational structures may have to be revised to facilitate the flow of evaluative feedback. Workers as well as managers become participants in the evaluative process. By this time the foundation is laid for future development of internal evaluation capability. Formal processes are established to identify information needs and to describe how the internal evaluation system should be designed. In addition, senior managers recognize the need to plan internal evaluation as an integral part of the organization.

Stage 3: Goal Evaluation

When sound systematic evaluation is available, it is possible to build management control capability that takes advantage of the data collected for use at the operational level. At the goal evaluation stage, organizations begin to design an internal evaluation capability that is relevant to their mission and goals. The internal evaluation information is mainly comparative ("Is this what should be?"). Comparing actual with intended goal achievement is not the same thing as defining goals or measurable objectives and simply monitoring their attainment, which is a descriptive (not a comparative) activity. Progress to the goal evaluation stage requires a formal system for defining potential goals, negotiating reasonable and measurable goals among constituent groups, assessing managers' information needs, involving workers, and designing the data collection and reporting processes.

Stage 4: Effectiveness Evaluation

Beginning at this point, there is an effort to evaluate the effectiveness of the organization and its programs. To reach this stage, managers must define effectiveness criteria and methods for measuring whether the criteria were achieved. They will want to use internal evaluation information to diagnose why criteria are not met and how to improve performance through corrective action. By now senior and middle managers have become aware of their information needs. As a result, managers share responsibility with internal evaluators for the definition and use of evaluative information. Evaluative information begins to be managed as a corporate resource.

Stage 5: Efficiency Evaluation

At this stage managers establish criteria for measuring the efficiency of the organization and programs in converting inputs (e.g., money, staff, knowledge) into outputs (e.g., products, services). They improve their accounting, financial, and information systems to enable the use of a common metric across programs (e.g., cost per unit of service, cost per change in level of functioning). They use effectiveness information (stage 4) to attain high levels of efficiency without affecting materially the quality of the organization's programs. Managers take greater responsibility for the definition and use of evaluative information across the entire organization.

Stage 6: Strategic Benefit

The final stage is the evaluation of strategic benefit when the ultimate social costs and benefits of the products or services are assessed. Increasingly senior managers regard internal evaluation information as an essential strategic tool. They look outside the boundaries of their firm to the external environment. Taking a broader perspective, top management evaluates the strategic benefit of its investments in products or programs. Guided by their organization's mission and philosophy, they select those with the highest ratios of benefits to costs, measured both in terms of the organization and society.

SUMMARY

The behavioral theory of the organization challenges the notion that a manager makes decisions in a rational manner to maximize profits or maximize the value of public expenditures. Instead, a manager makes decisions in a climate of uncertainty while balancing competing goals and the interests of different stakeholders.

A manager must make decisions and also see that the organization makes decisions effectively. The types of decisions vary from one organizational level of decision making to another. Senior managers are responsible for strategic decisions, middle managers for management control decisions, and frontline managers for operational control decisions. Internal evaluation must be responsive to the different information requirements at each of these management levels.

Decision making under conditions of uncertainty often leads to information overload. One way managers can cope with this situation is to invest in management support systems. Internal evaluation is one management support system that can help with every phase of the decision-making process.

The developmental model of internal evaluation capability explains how internal evaluation tends to grow in stages. Developing the capacity for systematic evaluation marks the true beginning of a useful internal evaluation capability. Subsequent stages include the capability to evaluate goals, effectiveness, efficiency, and strategic benefits.

EXERCISES

1. Describe the major differences between the economic theory of the organization and the behavioral theory. Which theory fits your organization better? Illustrate.

2. Explain why Nobel laureate Herbert Simon considered managing to be synonymous with the process of decision making. How does internal evaluation support managers during the process of decision making? How does internal evaluation improve the *organization's* ability to make decisions under conditions of uncertainty?

3. Imagine you are working in Willie Wampum's chocolate factory, in charge of hand-decorating exotic truffles. Your supervisor calls you aside and tells you that the Wampum internal evaluation unit will be evaluating the production of hand-decorated exotic truffles for the next three months. The supervisor tells you the internal evaluators consider pink flamingo motifs a 10 and the Jackson Pollock splatter look (your specialty) a 3 at best. How might the presence of the internal evaluation team affect you? Your truffles? Why?

4. Interview the manager in your organization, and summarize your observations in a brief report:
   (a) What are the usual sources of the manager's information?
   (b) What types of decisions does the manager usually make? What proportion are programmed decisions? Nonprogrammed decisions?

(c) Using Figure 2.2 as a guide, determine attributes of the types of information this manager finds useful for decision making.
(d) What stage of internal evaluation capability does the organization have? Give the reasons for your conclusions.
(e) Describe the organization briefly in terms of the organizational factors that might affect developing or using internal evaluation.

3

The Process of Internal Evaluation

This chapter outlines the essential toolbox of the internal evaluator by describing the steps in the internal evaluation process. These are the tools used for each internal evaluation study. If users' information needs remained the same, if programs and organizations never changed, and if internal evaluators always designed perfect evaluations, this chapter would not be needed. But such situations are merely wishful thinking. Even in the most stable environments, internal evaluators must understand and master the evaluation process. This mastery is necessary for avoiding pitfalls and disasters and absolutely essential for implementing responsive and relevant evaluations.

The chapter begins by presenting a model of internal evaluation consulting. This model shows internal evaluators how to exercise positive roles and form good working relationships with managers and staff, support managers with useful information, and tailor the internal evaluation process to the practical and political realities of organizational life. Next, this chapter offers a framework for selecting evaluation methods matched to the evaluation capability of the organization. Finally, it gives suggestions for enhancing the dependability of internal evaluation information and for conducting ethical evaluations.

A MODEL FOR INTERNAL
EVALUATION CONSULTING

The internal evaluation consulting model presented here has its conceptual roots in exchange theory (Baggozi, 1979; Lovelock & Weinberg, 1984). The basis of exchange theory is that an exchange takes place when the persons involved in the exchange perceive that the benefits of the exchange outweigh its costs. For example, in a simple purchasing exchange a person trades money for a product. The exchange takes place because the person perceives that the value of the product exceeds the value of the money paid for it.

To develop an effective consulting strategy, internal evaluators first must understand the nature of the exchanges between themselves and

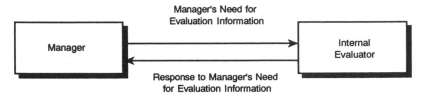

Figure 3.1. Simplified Model of an Exchange Between a Manager and an Internal Evaluator

their clients, who are usually managers. Figure 3.1 depicts the basic exchange: Managers need evaluation information, and internal evaluators provide a response to that need. If the internal evaluators cannot meet the managers' needs, then managers will not perceive enough benefit to make the exchange. According to exchange theory, an effective internal evaluation consulting relationship results from knowing managers' needs and their perceptions of benefits and costs. In establishing a consulting relationship, internal evaluators must be able to answer the question, "Who is the client?" Next, they must understand the client's point of view and the reality of the client's situation. Then internal evaluators must weigh evaluation strategies in light of the benefits and costs of various options available to the client.

There are several important implications of this model for internal evaluation consulting. Up to now, the focus of internal evaluation has been on setting objectives for the evaluation, selecting the methods, and implementing the study design. We know, however, that implementing even technically perfect evaluation studies seldom ensures that the information will be used by managers. Exchange theory and its concept of perceived benefits and costs shifts the focus to managers. In this model, internal evaluators use their consulting skills to identify the needs of managers and to facilitate relationships based upon meeting those needs. The central goal of this strategy is building a partnership between managers and internal evaluators. Internal evaluators must establish relationships with managers and staff based on mutually beneficial interactions. The business of internal evaluators is to make these relationships work.

The essential tasks for internal evaluators are: (a) identifying managers' needs, (b) having a response to those needs, and (c) verifying that the perceived benefits of the response outweigh its perceived costs. At the heart of this model is a move away from doing evaluations as an end in themselves, toward ensuring that evaluation information is used by managers successfully. Applying exchange theory, internal evaluation consulting will be dynamic and flexible, responding to changing needs. Internal evaluators will acknowledge their responsibility for providing ongoing support to managers, even after a study is complete. Finally, internal evaluators will actively market their services to managers, making them aware of internal evaluation's potential benefits.

THE INTERNAL EVALUATION CONSULTING PROCESS

The diagram in Figure 3.2 outlines the major phases in the internal evaluation consulting process. Table 3.1 presents the content and process objectives for each phase. In brief, once managers decide that they need assistance from internal evaluators in solving problems and making decisions, both parties must work together to diagnose the given problem and identify relevant evaluation strategies. During this process, internal evaluators carry the major responsibility for identifying the users of evaluation information, clarifying the problem and the purposes of the study, framing evaluation questions, and assessing the influence of organizational factors.

Following this, the managers and evaluators must agree on an evaluation plan suited to the problem in the light of organizational factors and constraints. After conducting the evaluation, the evaluators present the findings to the key audiences. Then managers (or managers and evaluators) create an action plan based on the findings. Finally, the evaluators monitor the implementation of the action plan and provide feedback to the managers about its progress.

INITIAL CONTACT

The initial contact gives the evaluator an opportunity to identify the key stakeholders, obtain background information, and assess the overall situation. In addition to this valuable information, the first contact affords the opportunity for intervention (Schein, 1969). Achieving the *process objectives* of the initial contact will influence the entire internal evaluation project. The evaluator should be keenly aware that meeting the demands of organizational politics, protocol, and process sets the stage for successful completion of the task.

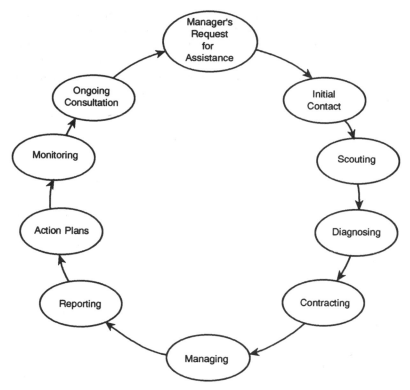

Figure 3.2. Major Phases in the Internal Evaluation Consulting Process

The initial contact is with the manager requesting help and the staff of the manager's unit. In larger organizations, however, a senior manager usually makes the request, and managers and staff in several departments will have meetings with the internal evaluator. Because managers and staff are often mistrustful of the prospect of evaluation, the initial contact provides the chance to develop rapport and dispel the stereotype of the "cold, analytical" evaluator discussed in Chapter 1.

Being an internal evaluator affects the emotional tone of this initial contact. Often a manager requests assistance because there are problems. A reality of organizational life is that asking help from an insider is very difficult and makes the manager feel vulnerable. The external person may seem more expert as well. The advantage of the insider is knowledge of the organization, its problems, and its players. The wise internal evaluator should take the time to make the manager and staff

Table 3.1

Content and Process Objectives for
Internal Evaluation Consulting Phases

Phase	Content Objectives	Process Objectives
Initial Contact	Identify evaluation users Obtain background info Assess situation	Develop rapport with managers & staff Dispel stereotypes of evaluators Establish credibility
Scouting	Clarify problem Clarify purposes Examine context Assess evaluation readiness Make preliminary diagnosis	Listen actively, probe Identify group norms & values Educate about evaluation Develop working relationship Confirm exchanges of benefits
Diagnosing	Analyze program materials Confirm stakeholders Confirm evaluation users Assess organizational factors Set priorities Appraise constraints Determine feasibility	Identify key program components Obtain perceptions of key stakeholders Strengthen working relationship Establish credibility Build trust Educate further about evaluation Agree on priorities of evaluation
Contracting	Confirm purpose Confirm design Establish timelines Assign duties Protect privacy Ensure data integrity Specify deliverables	Negotiate purpose & scope Negotiate design & methods Confirm mutual responsibilities Build support for the evaluation process Affirm standards of evaluation quality Negotiate deliverables Strengthen working relationship
Managing	Implement procedures Maintain schedule Maintain data quality Supervise staff Coordinate activities	Obtain support for data collection Motivate evaluation & program staff Resolve problems with data collection Strengthen trust Affirm credibility by producing results

(continued)

Table 3.1 (Continued)

Phase	Content Objectives	Process Objectives
Reporting	Validate methodology	Communicate clearly & concisely
	Communicate findings	Reaffirm expertise & credibility
	Identify key issues	Involve key stakeholders
	Define limitations	Stimulate discussion
	Clarify conclusions	Confront issues
	Offer recommendations	Facilitate resolving problems
Monitoring	Provide feedback	Monitor implementation
	Check milestones	Provide continuity
	Conduct reviews	Forge links to external resources
	Provide support	Facilitate resolving problems
	Revise program plans	Advocate change

aware of this knowledge, and use this as a platform to build credibility and trust.

SCOUTING

After the initial contact, the internal evaluator should develop a working relationship by obtaining firsthand information about the social and political context of the manager's unit. Scouting involves a quick appraisal of the unique culture of the unit or department by obtaining information from a reliable source or by observing it firsthand (Kolb & Frohman, 1970). These informal observations take place as part of a tour or walk-through of the premises, and during interviews. The evaluator should observe whether behavior and dress are formal or informal, whether staff participate in decisions, and whether certain values are held sacred and others are shunned. Although the internal evaluator should not be a chameleon, awareness of existing norms and values enables the evaluator to blend with the group and reduce unnecessary obstacles to effective interaction.

If the internal evaluator is new to the organization, or if the request takes the evaluator to an unfamiliar department, the evaluator should begin the scouting process by identifying the key managers on the organizational chart and then discovering their responsibilities, the product or service produced by the department, potential political problems, and other situations that may affect the department's managers and staff. The evaluator should make every effort to meet each key manager personally. During the interviews, the evaluator should concentrate on getting to know the executive by actively listening to the executive's opinions, and by probing. The evaluator should use the opportunity to build credibility and dispel any fears about the evaluation process. Once this is done, the evaluator should explore the manager's understanding of the problem.

The internal evaluator then clarifies the purpose of the evaluation. This affords an excellent opportunity for educating managers and staff about the uses of internal evaluation. The internal evaluator should probe by asking if the evaluation will be used for any of the following typical purposes. For example, will the evaluation be used for:

- providing an early warning on issues that could jeopardize the program?
- describing and assessing program users and the process of program delivery?
- rating the achievement of program milestones and goals?
- furnishing information to assist the program in attaining its goals?
- describing program results, both intended and unintended?
- evaluating the extent results are caused by program?
- weighing the costs and results of program alternatives?
- determining if the program is transferable to other sectors or organizations?

During the scouting phase, the internal evaluator assesses the program's readiness for evaluation. The internal evaluator listens and looks for the following positive signs:

- Managers want evaluation information to solve an identified problem.
- Managers and staff have clearly defined roles and responsibilities.
- Managers and staff have a positive attitude toward change.
- The program has a results-oriented culture.
- Managers provide capable leadership.
- The program design permits a flexible use of resources.
- Program politics do not subvert the evaluation process.

What do you do if the program manager and staff were burned by evaluators in the past, and now are hostile to your overtures? There are a number of ways of dealing with this situation. One is to start deliberately on a small evaluation project focusing on day-to-day activities, building up their confidence in you gradually. Projects with a fast payoff build credibility. Another is to deliver the benefits of evaluation to another program first, and then encourage the grapevine to spread the message to the reluctant program. Finally, have a trusted manager join the project team and ask that person to encourage the program to participate.

Skilled internal evaluators use the scouting activities to make a preliminary diagnosis of the problem and clarify the purposes of the evaluation. It enables the internal evaluator to assess the readiness of managers and staff to undertake the evaluation, and to formulate a preliminary diagnosis of the situation. Feedback about these early impressions gives both parties the chance to clarify their working relationship and come to a mutual understanding about the outcomes desired from the evaluation process.

DIAGNOSING

Up to this point, scouting has prepared the evaluator to begin a more inclusive diagnosis of the problem situation. The process of diagnosis involves the collection and analysis of relevant data (Kolb & Frohman, 1970; Schein, 1969). The evaluator explores possible solutions and provides feedback to the manager (and sometimes to the staff). The information is used by the manager and internal evaluator to define better the problem and the scope of the evaluation, set objectives for the evaluation, and plan the major steps of the study.

Diagnosing verifies that the problem expressed in the initial interview is valid. This is done by reviewing background written material and then meeting with persons or groups who are potential stakeholders in the evaluation. Stakeholders include potential users of evaluation information and those with an investment in the organization or unit involved in the study. Hegarty and Sporn (1988) recommend engaging stakeholders early because they have a different perspective, they have data the evaluator needs, and they can influence the evaluation positively if they are engaged, or negatively if they are ignored or threatened.

Although interviews are the staple diagnostic method, sometimes they are preceded by a short written survey to collect opinions anonymously. The diagnostic interviews focus on the participants' perceptions of the problem and surrounding issues. The internal evaluator must clarify who are the real stakeholders in the evaluation. The evaluator needs to know if there is agreement about the nature of the problem and the relative importance of the major issues.

Being an insider puts the internal evaluator in a strong position to question, to listen, and to clarify the problem. An internal evaluator is in a good place to judge the benefits and feasibility of the evaluation. At the end of diagnosis, the manager and internal evaluator should come to a decision of whether the proposed evaluation is feasible or not. They may decide to drop the evaluation, reformulate the questions, or further develop a working relationship.

Defining the Problem

Walter Hudson (1987) warns that selection and use of appropriate measures for internal evaluation must be guided by the far more critical criterion of "measuring the problem that you plan to solve." Measuring the problem depends greatly on (a) defining the problem in concrete terms, (b) using measuring tools that measure what the program intends to accomplish, and (c) using program methods that are capable of producing the desired results. Successful measurement in evaluation always centers upon the "clarification of and discrimination between the various types of questions which evaluations undertake to answer" (Scriven, 1980, p. 45).

Dillon (1984) observes that inadequate attention to the question-answer relationship leads to difficulties and poor performance in evaluations. In the internal evaluation setting, typical question-answer problems include: Managers and evaluators pose abstract and unanswerable questions, the evaluation never answers the questions posed, or the evaluation provides answers that ignore the questions originally posed. Dillon recommends four methods for improving this situation:

(1) *Classify.* Before specifying the question to study, classify the questions that the managers and evaluators are asking. This helps to discover and define the most important questions to evaluate.

(2) *Clarify.* Analyze potential questions by clarifying the assumptions behind each question and the assumptions of the person(s) posing the question. This step affirms the validity of the question and its rationale.

(3) *Construct.* Develop "dummy" answers to each question. Then have the dummy answers reviewed by managers and other stakeholders. This step helps determine the types of answers that present evaluative information in a meaningful and convincing manner.

(4) *Confirm.* Before presenting an answer, state the question. An answer may fit many questions, and evaluative questions have meaning only within a specific question-answer proposition.

Assessing the Organizational Context

The first two chapters have stressed the importance of organizational context for the practice of internal evaluation. Nowhere is this more evident than in the design of internal evaluation studies. David Clifford (1987) states that

> all aspects of the assessment of an organization's performance exist within the context of the organization's structure, which either hinders or facilitates that assessment. Structure determines what areas are assessed, what measures are used within each of those areas, how that information is communicated in the organization, what decision making settings it reaches, and how it is allowed to affect plans and decisions. Also, every one of the assessment mechanisms is itself an expression of the organization's structure. (p. 233)

When designing studies, evaluators may spend much time and resources guarding against statistical errors, but little effort and technical expertise to achieve excellence in understanding and structuring the organizational aspects of internal evaluations (Peach & Hirst, 1989). Considerable attention is given to controlling Type I errors (false assertion of a positive result) and Type II errors (failure to detect a positive result) through statistical and study design considerations (J. Cohen, 1977). However, threats to the validity and usefulness of results posed by practical or *Type III* errors are virtually ignored.

Spotting Type III Errors

Type III errors include asking the wrong questions, making the wrong types of claims, contaminating the evaluation with organizational or personal bias, and solving the right problem at the wrong time (Dunn, 1982). Internal evaluators must take responsibility for assessing Type III errors and the organizational variables that affect results, because inadequate organizational structuring can render technically competent work useless (Peach & Hirst, 1989).

Harrison (1987) presents a systematic approach for diagnosing organizational factors that may affect internal evaluation. Before designing a study, the internal evaluator answers the following questions:

How do the structural aspects of the organization interact with personal and group processes to affect programs and outcomes? When the cause-and-effect relationships of the core program methods are not well understood, precise assessment measures become suspect (Clifford, 1987). Fred Newman and his colleagues (Newman, Heverly, Rosen, Kopta, & Bedell, 1983; Newman, White, Zuskar, & Plaut, 1983) illustrate several ways behavioral and interpersonal variables can be measured and controlled. Evaluability assessment (Chapter 4) also is a useful tool in these situations.

Which actions of managers at each management level (i.e., line, middle, or top) influence programs and outcomes? Rino Patti (1983, 1987) provides detailed descriptions of the management activities associated with effectiveness at each management level. For example, senior managers require service effectiveness data for justifying service plans and budget submissions; program managers develop performance standards related to service effectiveness; and supervisors set performance targets with frontline staff.

How does the behavior of managers at the higher levels affect the behavior of managers and workers at the lower levels? Studies have suggested that the interaction styles of senior and lower-level managers affect the performance of workers and service outcomes (Graen, 1977). See Blanchard and Tager (1985) for specific ways of identifying the negative interaction styles of managers and solutions to correct them.

Is the organizational environment stable or volatile? Some organizations exist in extremely volatile environments. Because measures of desirable performance have multiple dimensions and relate to multiple stakeholders, the internal evaluator must be aware that different measures may be in conflict with some stakeholders (Clifford, 1987). In stable environments with a clear mission and a readiness to change, the process of internal evaluation is more readily accepted, especially for evaluating program effectiveness (Chapter 6). Radin (1987) and Sonnichsen (1988) make this same point when describing the development of internal evaluation within the FBI.

Assessing the Cost and Relative Merit of Evaluation Approaches

As part of the diagnosis, internal evaluators estimate the cost and relative merit of potential evaluation approaches. This step helps evaluators to propose feasible designs that have demonstrable benefits. In particular the internal evaluator should appraise the hard and soft benefits of the evaluation; the costs in dollars and in program staff time; and the organizational implications in terms of changes in forms and procedures, changes in job descriptions and compensation, impact on job status, and impact on group morale.

Developing a Terms of Reference

The diagnosis phase should end with the drafting of a Terms of Reference (TOR). The TOR is a detailed written description of the specifications for the evaluation. The purpose of the Terms of Reference is to provide a clear description of the study requirements so the internal evaluator can work with program managers and staff to develop an evaluation plan that meets the users' information needs. A good TOR ensures that both the program managers and the internal evaluators have a common framework for negotiating the goals, methods, and deliverables of the evaluation study. At the minimum, a good TOR should include the items outlined in Table 3.2.

CONTRACTING

Drafting the TOR gives managers and evaluators a chance to review the feasibility of the proposed study. If both parties agree to continue, they now begin the *contracting* phase of the internal evaluation consulting process. Internal evaluation contracts are psychological contracts rather than legal ones. They serve to clarify roles and expectations instead of being a legally binding arrangement between parties. Yet the internal evaluation contract is crucial because it builds trust by clearly communicating the internal evaluator's understanding of the manager's needs and by binding the two together through a set of mutually acceptable expectations. Thus the contract reduces the chances of resistance and sabotage frequently associated with evaluation studies.

Contracting imparts clarity to an inherently ambiguous process. In formulating a written contract, the internal evaluator and manager strengthen their working relationship by confirming the purpose and scope of the evaluation, specifying study methods and time lines, negotiating the financial and staff resources required, and agreeing on the deliverables (e.g., presentations, reports). The contract also offers the opportunity to specify the responsibilities and procedures for protecting the quality and confidentiality of the evaluation data. Of necessity,

Table 3.2
Outline for Internal Evaluation Terms of Reference

- *Introduction.* Who wants the evaluation? What is the background of the program, including its clients and program model? Who are the major stakeholders in the program? What are the major benefits expected from the evaluation?
- *Users of the Evaluation Information.* Who are the key users of evaluation information?
- *Purposes of the Evaluation.* What are the major purposes of the evaluation?
- *Evaluation Questions.* What are the essential and secondary evaluation questions that the study should answer?
- *Study Parameters.* What are the mandatory data requirements, sources of data, expertise, geographic restrictions, or sensitive issues that the study must address?
- *Preliminary Design.* What evaluation design seems feasible?
- *Staffing.* What program and internal evaluation staff will take part in the study? What tasks will be their responsibility?
- *Confidentiality Issues.* Are there any special confidentiality issues?
- *Deliverables.* What are the due dates for interim and final reports? How will they be presented (e.g., oral briefing, written report, audio-visual presentation)?
- *Dissemination.* What is the preliminary plan for disseminating results, including the composition of the major audiences, the method(s) of dissemination, and the timing of dissemination?
- *Time Line.* When will the major study phases begin and end?
- *Constraints.* Are there special constraints (e.g., budget, staff resources, timing) that affect the design and/or implementation of the study?

---

internal evaluation contracts are specific to every situation and every organization, but when negotiating a contract, evaluators should consider the items found in Table 3.3.

For many internal evaluators and managers alike, defining the time and resources needed for an evaluation is a very difficult process. A fundamental problem is the way the internal evaluation process is structured. External evaluators are hired to undertake a well-defined job; the resources required are specified in a written contract. The contract may be terminated after a notice period if either party isn't satisfied. In many organizations, neither managers nor internal evaluators

Table 3.3
Outline for Internal Evaluation Contract

- *Purposes of the Evaluation.* What are the major purposes of the study?
- *Evaluation Information Users.* Who are the key users of the study information?
- *Evaluation Questions.* What are the key questions answered by the study?
- *Synopsis of Evaluation Design and Methodology.* In brief, what are the design and the methods used in the study?
- *Management of Study.* Who is the study team leader, and what are the lines of authority and accountability?
- *Steering Committee and Liaison.* Who belongs to the study steering committee? Who provides liaison with the program and the internal evaluation unit?
- *Staffing.* Which internal evaluation and program personnel are staffing the study?
- *Special Staffing Resources.* What special technical resources or consultants does the study need? Who will recruit them and pay for them?
- *Responsibilities.* What are the responsibilities of study staff? Who will review and approve the deliverables?
- *Time Line.* What are the start and finish dates for the major study milestones and phases?
- *Tasks.* What is the work plan and schedule of tasks?
- *Cooperation.* What specific cooperation is expected from program staff? Which manager will ensure that the expected cooperation occurs?
- *Data Quality Control.* What procedures are staff expected to follow to ensure the accuracy of the data they collect?
- *Confidentiality.* What are the specific confidentiality safeguards required by the study (e.g., informed client consent, staff oath of confidentiality)?
- *Deliverables.* What deliverables will the study produce (e.g., interim and final briefings, presentations, reports)?
- *Ownership.* Who (e.g., program, evaluation unit) will own specified items such as deliverables, data, and measures?
- *Monitoring the Implementation of Study Recommendations.* Who will have responsibility for monitoring the implementation of study recommendations?
- *Limitations.* Are there any constraints or limitations that affect the study design or deliverables?
- *Early Termination of the Study.* Under what circumstances can the study be stopped?

have these safeguards. The internal evaluator's role may be murky, the length of the evaluator's engagement may be open-ended, the costs of the evaluation may be seen as fictional "funny money," and the manager may have no recourse if the evaluation doesn't proceed according to plan.

If the previous steps are followed, contracting just formalizes the understanding among parties. A key element, however, is recognizing that contracting for internal evaluation is not the same as hiring external consultants. Contracting for internal evaluation acknowledges the manager's responsibility for the evaluation. Unless there is clear ownership of the evaluation by the manager and his or her staff, enthusiasm and cooperation are likely to flag. Ownership translates into defining tasks and responsibilities of managers and staff, as well as those of the internal evaluator.

MANAGING

At this point, the internal evaluator begins *managing* the evaluation. The procedures specified in the evaluation plan must be implemented and deadlines observed.

Forming a Steering Committee

The steering committee may act as a senior management committee, meeting periodically to review work prepared by the study team and program managers. It may act as an action committee, meeting regularly to define tasks and manage the evaluation process. The structure of the organization, its lines of authority, and the available time of senior managers influence the design of the steering committee.

Selecting a Study Team

The study team has direct responsibility for the study. The team is small, consisting of between 4 and 10 members, depending on the size of the study. The study team usually includes managers and staff from the program being evaluated, a senior manager from another program, and the internal evaluators assigned to the study. One of the senior managers leads the study team. This person should have professional competence, influence, knowledge of how to get things done within the organization, and commitment to the evaluation study. The team leader chairs team meetings, drafts meeting agendas, assigns responsibilities, ensures that tasks are completed by their deadlines, and disseminates study deliverables to key managers and audiences in the organization. The study team members should report directly to the study team leader. The team members should possess specialized skills relevant to the evaluation, a strong commitment to the evaluation process, and the ability to work as part of a team. They have the responsibility for carrying out their assigned tasks on time, coordinating their work with other team members, attending team meetings as required, and keeping program information confidential. The following are some tips on how to build an effective study team:

- Keep teams small.
- Acknowledge team members' need for high performance.
- Reward both team leaders and team members.
- Focus on people, not methodology.
- Keep a skills inventory of team members.
- Make use of project management tools to create benchmarks of success.

As members of a study team, internal evaluators facilitate group interaction and provide technical assistance. They provide staffing support to the team leader by contributing to team agendas, defining tasks and study phases, monitoring study progress, spotting problems, and drafting progress reports. They facilitate group interaction by focusing on the major evaluation issues specified in the TOR and evaluation contract, providing support for individual team members during group meetings, and recognizing the contributions of team members.

Asserting Management Control

Achieving a high quality evaluation while containing costs is a major goal of managing internal evaluations. This demands finely honed project management strategies. The cornerstone for these strategies is the internal evaluation contract that specifies the deliverables right at the start of the study. Clearly specifying deliverables is important because additional resources rarely are available for a study with a larger scope. If changes are necessary once the study has begun, the working relationship established during the contracting phase will aid in arriving at an acceptable negotiated agreement.

A management system is necessary for ensuring the technical adequacy of the evaluation and the quality of the deliverables. A combination of management by objectives (Chapter 5) and quality reviews (Chapter 4) often is used by the steering committee and the study team to ensure quality, track the achievement of milestones, and contain costs.

Meeting Study Deadlines

A persistent problem in managing internal evaluations is meeting study deadlines. Often approvals from various committees are slow in coming, budgets or staff resources are reduced, or a study is delayed by the sudden transfer of a senior member of the steering committee to another assignment. The credibility of the internal evaluator and the successful completion of an evaluation study depend on meeting study deadlines. Not all delays are avoidable, but internal evaluators may use several proven strategies to reduce their impact.

The first strategy is to specify the elapsed time for the study and to start the clock running *after* receiving the necessary approvals. In other words, instead of stating in the evaluation contract, "The study will begin on March 1st and end on May 31st," rephrase it to read, "The study will be completed within three months of receiving all approvals." The second strategy is to include a contingency clause in the contract that states the study will be completed on a certain date "unless unforeseen circumstances cause unavoidable delays." The third strategy is to include a clause in the contract that the study schedule may be modified if "unforeseen circumstances force delays of more than X weeks."

Although these strategies may help avoid responsibility for delays, the credibility of internal evaluators suffers irrespective of who causes the delays. For these reasons, internal evaluators must carefully monitor study progress and be quick to draw delays to the study team leader's attention. This individual should use his or her influence and knowledge of the organizational structure to keep the study on schedule. Alternatively, the study team leader should develop fallback strategies that modify some elements of the evaluation design if the schedule deteriorates too far. For example, a telephone survey may replace a mailed questionnaire if study delays become excessive.

REPORTING

Reporting evaluation findings is the next phase in the consulting process. Reporting affords the opportunity to improve the utilization of evaluations by involving key stakeholders, stimulating discussion, confronting issues, and providing an opportunity for resolving problems. To take full advantage of the opportunity, internal evaluators first must reaffirm their expertise and credibility by reviewing the study methodology and quality control safeguards. Next, they must present their findings clearly and concisely in a way that matches the types of information needed by managers and that considers management and data assessment styles.

Types of Information Needed by Managers

Understanding the major attributes of information needed by managers (Chapter 2) provides the guidelines for reporting evaluation findings. Figure 2.2 shows that the types of information vary according to management level within the organization. Managers at the frontline level prefer quantitative, detailed, descriptive information; middle managers want quantitative, aggregate, analytic information; and senior managers need qualitative, highly summarized information identifying trends. The mode of reporting also differs by management level: Line managers need numerical and text data reports; middle managers prefer reports that include plots or graphs that identify exceptions; and senior managers prefer oral briefings and presentations portraying information graphically. Research has shown that management style and data assessment styles also influence the reporting of evaluation information to managers.

Identifying Management Style

Michael Driver and Alan Rowe (1979) identified four types of managers, characterized by the way they use information to make decisions: the flexible manager, who depends on experience and intuition to make decisions and personal contacts to enhance implementation; the decisive manager, who makes rapid "satisficing" decisions after reviewing summary information and the available alternatives; the hierarchical manager, who reviews detailed information from many sources, taking time to arrive at "optimizing" decisions; and the integrative manager, who uses logic to assess information and decide among alternatives.

Recognizing Data Assessment Style

Managers also have different styles of assessing data. For example, one middle manager may use exceptional reports and summary information to make management control decisions. Another middle manager may also use selected detailed reports to get at the crux of the problems while making use of strategic summary reports to ensure that the changes are in keeping with the directions of the overall organization.

Phased Reporting

One of the hallmarks of an effective internal evaluation system is that it provides the information managers need *at the right time* for decision making. Conversely, no single factor shatters the credibility of internal evaluators faster than not meeting deadlines. Experienced internal evaluators use phased reporting to ensure the timely delivery of information. The phased approach divides studies into distinct phases, and evaluators make reports at the end of each phase (Winberg, 1986). In this way, managers can receive information without waiting for the completion of the full study.

MONITORING

The final phase in the internal evaluation consulting process is monitoring the implementation of recommendations and action plans originating from the evaluation study. The internal evaluator checks the achievement of milestones and provides feedback about progress during periodic review meetings. The internal evaluator provides technical support during the implementation of program changes and assists program managers in revising program plans if necessary.

The internal evaluator advocates change but provides continuity while the program undergoes transition. Exercising the evaluator's linking role, the internal evaluator helps the program to forge links with outside resources. The internal evaluator facilitates the solution of problems by motivating staff and providing technical support.

SELECTING EVALUATION METHODS

The developmental theory of program evaluation capability presented in Chapter 2 described the six stages of progressively greater capacity for internal evaluation. In the first stage, evaluations are used in an isolated fashion to meet the information needs of individual managers and project teams. True internal evaluation begins at the second stage, when the systematic collection and reporting of evaluation information supports managers' problem solving and decision making. It then progresses through the stages of goal evaluation, effectiveness evaluation, and efficiency evaluation and culminates with strategic benefits evaluation.

According to this theory, each higher stage of evaluation capability depends on the organizational and evaluation structures and processes established in the previous stage. The choice of evaluation methods depends largely on the organization's stage of evaluation capability and the information needs of managers. As an illustrative guide to using this method, Table 3.4 presents the major management questions matched to evaluation methods for each level of evaluation capability. Descriptions of systematic evaluation methods appear in Chapter 4; goal evaluation methods in Chapter 5; effectiveness evaluation methods in Chapter 6; efficiency evaluation methods in Chapter 7; and strategic benefits evaluation in Chapter 8.

ENSURING THE QUALITY OF
INTERNAL EVALUATION DATA

A paradox underlies the issue of data dependability for internal evaluation. In the words of Fred Newman and his colleagues (Newman, White, et al., 1983) the paradox is that "the greatest responsibility for data collection and processing is bestowed on frontline staff, while the greatest responsibility for assuring the reliability and validity of data is given to supervisory or middle-level staff" (p. 63).

Given that data collected by frontline employees are used by persons at all levels of the organization for internal evaluation purposes, this raises the question: How are internal evaluation data used for organizational control? Subordinates want to know how the data will affect their position in the organization, and managers want to know if the data collected by persons who may be affected by the results will

Table 3.4

Management Questions and Evaluation Methods at
Each Stage of Evaluation Capacity

Stage	Management Questions	Evaluation Methods
Systematic Evaluation	Who needs this program? Who needs it the most?	Needs Assessment
	Who uses this program?	Program Utilization
	What are the program components? What are their causal relationships?	Evaluability Assessment
	What are the levels of client acceptance and client satisfaction with this program?	Client Satisfaction
	What is the quality of the products or services produced by this program?	Quality Assurance
	How well does this program rate against accepted standards?	Self-Study
Goal Evaluation	What are the goals of this program? What are the indicators of goal achievement?	Goal Definition
	What is the program plan and budget?	Budgeting
	Are income and expenditure meeting budget targets?	Budgeting
	Are key program and organizational goals being met?	Management By Objectives
	How well are program efforts and outcomes meeting targets?	Goal Attainment Scaling
	Are program milestones being met?	Program Monitoring
Effectiveness Evaluation	Is this a good program? Is the program producing the intended outcomes?	Monitoring of Outcome Indicators
	What are the areas for improvement?	Monitoring of Outcome Indicators
	Is this program better or worse than a competing program?	Comparative Outcome evaluation
	What are the costs for a given level of outcome?	Cost-Effectiveness Evaluation
	What are the problems common to *all* programs and their solutions?	Quality Assurance Reviews

Efficiency Evaluation	What programs are inefficient?	Managerial Accounting
	Is the program meeting its goals for the quantity of program activities?	Monitor Efficiency Goals
	What problems are affecting efficiency? How can they be corrected?	Internal & Operational Audits
	What are the relationships among income, costs, and program outputs?	Quantitative Modeling
Strategic Benefits Evaluation	What are the characteristics of the external environment?	Environmental Scan
	What markets are being reached by the program?	Strategic Market Analysis
	What organizations support the program?	Network Analysis
	What is the future demand for services?	Forecasting
	What are the long-term benefits and costs of the program?	Benefit/Cost Analysis
	Are the program's benefits being distributed fairly?	Equity Analysis
	Are the intended stakeholders receiving the benefits of the program?	Political Rationality Analysis

be dependable. The practical answer to these questions involves establishing a process of data quality control.

Data quality control is a primary concern of any evaluation process, whether the evaluation is external or internal. Newman and his colleagues suggest four key steps for decreasing the bias of internal evaluation data, and increasing their reliability and validity (Newman, White, et al., 1983). These steps involve (a) devising a plan for data collection, (b) pilot testing, (c) training, and (d) assigning responsibility for data collection. Each of these steps will be described briefly.

Data collection plan. The written plan is essential as it provides a general blueprint for data collection as well as details of the process of data collection and monitoring. The plan also should provide explicit instructions for recording and entering data. The written plan should be supplemented with a flowchart diagram specifying the data to be collected by each staff person, the sequence of collection, and the name of the person responsible for monitoring the quality of the data. It is essential that the responsible person be sufficiently senior to have clout, although the actual monitoring may be delegated to a person more junior. Finally, the plan should propose strategies for dealing with potential problems in data collection. In some organizations, a monthly report is enough to exert sufficient pressure, whereas in other situations specific penalties may need to be imposed.

Pilot testing. The purpose of pilot testing is to assess (a) the adequacy of the data in meeting information needs, (b) the reliability of data collection procedures, and (c) the feasibility of the data collection process. First of all, through discussions with managers and staff, pilot testing verifies that the right data are being collected to provide the desired information. It establishes that the data can be collected accurately. Finally, pilot testing provides feedback about the costs and staff efforts required to collect the data, the overall feasibility of the process, and recommendations for making data collection more practical.

Training. Training in the collection of data usually begins during the pilot testing phase to assess how much and what type of training are appropriate. Training often can be integrated into other ongoing activities, such as individual or peer supervision, or quality control workshops. Evaluating the effectiveness of the training is essential. Special care should be taken during training to confirm that definitions and instructions are understood and interpreted the same way. Because staff in each department or location are likely to have a unique frame of reference, trainers should be alert to identifying and resolving such differences in interpretations.

Assigning responsibility for data collection. One person should have clear authority to coordinate the data collection process. In practice, this person operates in conjunction with a steering or advisory committee composed of key persons representing the relevant parts of the organization. The advisory committee ensures that the necessary political and staff support will be received for the data collection system. The committee also provides a reality check concerning the feasibility of the data collection procedures, and a problem-solving resource useful in diagnosing and resolving data collection problems.

ETHICAL CONSIDERATIONS

Ethics is a topic of growing concern as evaluators try to ensure that their studies are used for worthwhile purposes and that the welfare of all participants is protected. Internal evaluators face two major forms of ethical issues. First, by virtue of being an employee of an organization, the internal evaluator may be torn between loyalty to the organization and meeting standards of professional conduct (Korn, 1982). Kay Adams (1985) identifies the ethical dilemmas internal evaluators face as members of an organization. These include pressures to emphasize positive findings, to avoid evaluations that question basic assumptions or have the potential to produce negative findings, to provide a "ritual function" rather than encourage managers to use evaluation results, and to abuse their access to privileged information.

Example: In a report of evaluation results for an external funding source, the superintendent of a large school district pressured the director of evaluation to downplay the negative findings. Although the evaluator won the battle to present the negative findings, the evaluator was excluded from meetings, denied travel requests, and given low-status assignments (Adams, 1985, p. 53).

Many of the above problems may be traced to the multiple roles required of internal evaluators (Sieber, 1980). By following the internal evaluation consulting model described in earlier in this chapter, most of these dilemmas may be avoided. For example, by using exchange theory internal evaluators will identify the benefits of the evaluation for the managers before beginning the evaluation, and be less vulnerable to pressure and "payoffs." Scouting will give internal evaluators and managers the chance to clarify their working relationship and come to a mutual understanding about the outcomes desired from the evaluation process. Assessing the organizational context helps identify and correct sources of bias. Contracting helps clarify the nature of the psychological contract between evaluators and managers as well as the specifications for the evaluation. The presence of a steering committee helps build a support base and avoid ethical conflicts by working with influential persons in the organization. Finally, phased reporting provides an early warning to managers and a "no surprises" approach to the final report.

Second, the process of conducting evaluation studies within organizations may pose unique ethical problems (Attkisson, Hargreaves, Horowitz, & Sorensen, 1978; Ciarlo, 1982; Hargreaves, 1982). Some of these were touched upon in the discussion of data dependability in the previous section.

Example: Newman, Hunter and Irving (1987) describe ethical abuses when evaluating program effectiveness. These include:

- using scales that are insensitive to changes in the target population;
- using scales that are not useful in all the settings in which they are applied;
- permitting the staff to make inaccurate ratings; and
- using the data to punish staff.

The study design, data collection instruments, study procedures, and use of outcome data may jeopardize the well-being of participants and staff. This is particularly true in situations where a person has committed an offense and the persons collecting the data have the "duty to warn" in keeping with the Tarasoff decision (Kimmel, 1988). For reasons such as these, internal evaluators should use standard ethical safeguards, such as informed consent, that define the study procedures and potential risks and benefits. Ethical safeguards include limiting deception by informing clients about the possibility of withholding a program or being assigned to an alternative program (i.e., attention control group). If deception is used by assigning a client to a placebo control group, then the clients are asked for post hoc consent and they receive debriefing to minimize unintended consequences (e.g., mistrust, low self-esteem). In many organizations, ethical concerns prevent using control groups, and alternate strategies must be employed.

SUMMARY

Internal evaluators must master the internal evaluation consulting process to avoid pitfalls and ensure high quality evaluations. The internal evaluation consulting model draws its conceptual roots from exchange theory. The core of the model is developing a strong relationship between internal evaluators and managers based on meeting managers' information needs in a way that the manager clearly perceives that the benefits of evaluation outweigh its costs. The business of internal evaluators is to make these relationships work.

The consulting model defines the major steps in the internal evaluation consulting process, including the task and process objectives for each phase. The steps of initial contact, scouting, and diagnosis clarify the purpose of the evaluation and strengthen the relationships among participants in the evaluation, leading to contracting an evaluation study. The process of managing the study is next, followed by the reporting of evaluation findings, and then monitoring the implementation of recommendations and action plans. Next, the model uses the developmental theory of program evaluation capability (Chapter 2) to provide guidelines for selecting evaluation methods. The essence of using this approach is (a) recognizing the developmental stage of the organization, (b) understanding the questions of managers that reflect their information needs, and (c) selecting methods that meet their needs within the evaluation capability of the organization. The model also incorporates methods for ensuring the quality of data by (a) devising a plan for data collection, (b) pilot testing, (c) training, and (d) assigning responsibility for data collection. Finally, the model addresses ethical issues that affect internal evaluation consulting.

EXERCISES

After reviewing written material about the organization, arrange to meet with the manager to discuss the questions that will be the focus of your hypothetical evaluation efforts. Arrange an interview with key program staff, either individually or in a group, to discuss your assignment.

1. Describe the culture of (a) the organization and (b) the program. In what ways does it facilitate or hinder internal evaluation?

2. What are the major problems faced by the program from the perspectives of the manager and the staff?

3. What problems do the manager and staff want evaluated in your hypothetical evaluation? What are the major evaluation questions they want answered?

4. Draft a Terms of Reference (TOR) for the hypothetical study. Circulate this to the manager and key staff for comments.

5. Given the evaluation questions contained in the TOR, and your assessment of the evaluation capability of the organization, what evaluation methods seem most suitable for this study?

6. What are the major ethical issues faced by an evaluation study in this program? What strategies do you suggest to resolve them?

4

Developing Systematic Internal Evaluation

Systematic internal evaluation is one of the key elements of good management. Sound decisions about the performance of programs and the overall agency depend on accurate evaluative information together with good judgment. Systematic internal evaluation provides information for planning and improving program operations. It enables potential problems to be spotted rapidly. Managers benefit from having timely information, the organization benefits from increased efficiency, and clients benefit from greater effectiveness.

True internal evaluation begins at the systematic evaluation stage. At this point, the organization's information needs have been analyzed. Internal evaluators facilitate this process by involving senior managers, administrators, middle and line managers, and frontline workers. Through this process, they reach common agreement on the content, categories, and systems for data collection and reporting. This permits standardized descriptions of an organization in terms of inputs and operations. Given this information, evaluations of a monitoring nature can take place. Managers can record their plans, then check to see if reality matches their expectations. Then they can make adjustments to resources and program operations. They also can conduct simple but reliable analyses of baseline operating data, such as monitoring service workloads and trend analysis.

At the systematic evaluation level there is a focus on internal regulation and control. The management and evaluation goals at this stage are to develop routine monitoring procedures (to flag errors and deficiencies that threaten operations) and to detect deviations from established plans.

Internal evaluation data assist the organization in meeting requirements for ongoing evaluative information required for regulatory compliance and survival: meeting internal and external reporting requirements; documenting client/consumer needs; describing programs and services; collecting information needed to set program priorities; planning programs and budgets; obtaining and maintaining financial support; identifying and allocating financial and staff resources;

monitoring staff effort and allocation of resources; monitoring income and expenditures; finding unit costs; establishing fees and billing rates; and relating to community planning groups.

At this level, the organization also uses systematic internal evaluation data to monitor its service delivery processes and to help managers understand the organization's activities: providing statistical summaries to keep all organizational activities visible, and therefore more manageable; conducting evaluative studies to examine client entry requirements, referral patterns, units of service rendered, and factors that influence service delivery and channel client demand; and submitting findings from client studies to funders to meet accountability requirements.

The following sections describe a variety of practical methods for systematic internal evaluation: needs assessment, program utilization studies, evaluability assessment, systematic program monitoring, consumer/client satisfaction studies, internal auditing, quality assurance, and self-study.

NEEDS ASSESSMENT

The internal evaluation consulting process described in Chapter 3 supplies a rapid appraisal of problems and their organizational context. When the situation demands it, needs assessment provides a systematic procedure for setting priorities and making decisions about programs and the allocation of resources (Witkin, 1984). There are many definitions of need and needs assessment, but the consensus seems to be that needs assessment is a formal analytic tool for problem identification that reveals needs in terms of gaps between current results and desired outcomes, identifies unique strengths and areas of excellence, sets priorities among needs, and selects the needs to be changed (Kaufman, 1982). Kaufman and English (1979) further distinguish between internal and external needs assessment. Internal needs assessment restricts the analysis to the boundaries of the organization; it is the type frequently used by internal evaluators. Needs assessment is an integral part of the organizational planning and evaluation cycle and an important component of internal evaluation (Rothman, 1980).

There are numerous models of needs assessment, and no single method seems suitable to all purposes and organizational contexts.

Kamis (1981, pp. 28-32) describes four common approaches: (a) directly assessing needs through a survey; (b) interviewing key informants; (c) inferring needs from ongoing use of services; and (d) inferring needs from known associations between social area characteristics and the prevalence of social and health problems. Educational needs assessments, however, often use surveys of goal preferences, indicators such as standardized test scores, and group processes (Witkin, 1984). The term *organizational assessment* (Lawler, Nadler, & Cammann, 1980) is used sometimes to describe techniques for assessing organizational performance. Organizational assessment relies on methods to assess individual need, group need, and quality of work life.

Social Indicator Analysis

Social indicators are descriptive statistics that may be used to draw inferences about the characteristics of persons with specific needs, the extent of those needs, and the relationship between different needs. Indicators, however, cannot set priorities among needs, specify the causes of problems, suggest solutions, or show if a program or intervention has been successful. Social indicators are often misidentified exclusively with social statistics such as census data. Cochran (1979) identifies three major types of social indicators: social statistics describing population differences and economic indicators; indicators that include implications of economic and geographic data; and subjective quality-of-life indicators.

Data for social indicator analysis usually come from secondary data sources (e.g., public reports and public-use computer tapes, such as those produced by the U.S. Bureau of the Census, Statistics Canada, and the National Center for Health Statistics) and reports of national, regional, state/provincial, and local agencies. The scope and the sources of social indicator data depend on the objectives of the study and the types of data that will be the best indicators of need. Common indicators include demographic characteristics (e.g., age, gender, marital status); health indicators (prevalence and incidence rates of disease, hospital admission rates); education indicators (enrollment and dropout rates); criminal justice indicators (arrest rates and crime patterns); and housing indicators (occupation rates by owners and renters).

Example: A local planning group in a large urban area wanted to gain a better understanding of the social needs of youths in the ages of transition from youth to adulthood (16 to 24 years of age). Census data provided information about the population trends for this age group, and epidemiological data from government agencies and treatment centers provided estimates of the prevalence of mental health needs. Social indicators data on 13 factors (e.g., crime rates, school dropout rates, poverty levels) enabled comparisons of risk for various parts of the planning area.

In many organizations, the internal evaluator may conduct social indicator studies using data drawn from personnel records, indicators of productivity (e.g., sales calls, sales, quality control data), and products or services delivered. The problem with these data is twofold. First, usually they are collected for specific purposes by departments and are not intended to be standardized for use across the organization. Second, the types of indicators chosen in the first place may reflect the bias of the original users to justify a certain management decision. Data from existing files may be supplemented with standardized self-administered questionnaires to obtain quality-of-work-life data. Instruments similar to the Organization Assessment Instrument (Van de Ven & Ferry, 1980) and those in the Michigan Quality of Work Program (Seashore, Lawler, Mirvis, & Cammann, 1983) provide individual and group social indicator information about such factors as personal background, job characteristics, adequacy of training and skills for the job, quality of work life, characteristics of the work group, group behavior, and group performance.

Social indicator analysis studies have the advantage of making use of existing data sources. Although public data are available at nominal cost, social indicator studies in practice tend to become expensive because of the effort required to analyze and synthesize this wealth of data. This cost may be averted by carefully selecting the indicators used in the study.

If the data collected are complex, if composite indices are created, and if comparisons are made with other communities, the analysis may be time-consuming and require a high level of technical competence. Social indicator needs assessments are prone to problems of interpretation. For example, there is the tendency to generalize the statistical rates and averages to the range of persons working in an organization or living in a community, or to infer that the population characteristics cause certain needs. The objections to social indicator studies usually can be eliminated through the use of confirming information from other types of needs assessment studies.

Needs Assessment Surveys

Needs assessment surveys are usually conducted with consumers, clients, or employees of an organization. They are the most efficient method for needs assessment. A well-designed survey provides a scientifically credible method for directly obtaining data about the desired population. The survey is particularly useful for providing detailed information, verifying data collected by other methods, and investigating important needs and their potential impact. On the negative side, surveys tend to be more expensive than alternative approaches, and for some types of organizations there may be serious problems with self-report and response bias.

Mail surveys should include a random sample of people living within the capture area. The sample may be stratified by factors such as census tract, age, sex, race, or economic status. Respondents are nearly always anonymous. Another option is the *telephone survey,* which yields a higher response rate than a mailed questionnaire. The telephone survey maintains many of the advantages of a face-to-face interview at a fraction of the cost (Lavrakas, 1987). Unlike mail surveys and personal interviews, telephone surveys permit a high degree of control that ensures valid sampling and standardized interviewing. They also provide information more quickly than these other two methods.

Example: A large multinational organization had their internal evaluators assess training needs by a survey. There were three major steps to the survey: (a) a panel of potential trainees or experts identified training areas; (b) a questionnaire was developed, and survey participants rated each question with respect to the level of current performance, the level of desired performance, and the willingness to be trained; and (c) training priorities were set, taking the above information and training costs into account (Misanchuk, 1984). The survey saved training resources formerly wasted when needs were identified in supervision sessions or on the basis of skills without considering willingness to be trained.

Interviewing

Interviews are perhaps the most popular technique for needs assessments. The interview is a very flexible method for asking direct questions and then obtaining clarification or elaboration of responses on the spot. Structured interviews ask a series of highly specific questions usually derived from a theoretical model. Unstructured interviews are less specific and ask broad questions about needs and concerns.

Interviews are an effective method for collecting needs assessment data. They permit the interviewer to develop a personal relationship with respondents that facilitates candid responses to sensitive issues. With some groups of individuals (e.g., illiterate or ethnic groups), personal interviews produce a better response rate than mail surveys. Persons indigenous to the group may be used as interviewers.

Key Informant Interviews

This method involves selecting 10 to 15 knowledgeable persons and then asking these key informants to offer their perceptions on the needs of various groups within the organization or in the community. Key informants are selected from a cross-section of informed people. An *internal* needs assessment may include key executives, department heads, policy and financial advisors, professional staff, and key employees. An external needs assessment for a human service agency or school board, for example, may include persons such as members of community planning and coordinating groups, key state or provincial funders, municipal planners, local health and education officials, and previous clients or students and their family members.

Organizational Group Techniques

Interviews may be conducted within the organization to collect data about issues such as worker satisfaction, quality of work life, and responses to changes in procedures. These interviews are usually one-to-one key informant interviews, but group interviews may be used to reduce time and cost.

The organizational *sensing interview* (Dunphy, 1981) is used for needs assessment purposes by internal evaluators. Sensing interviews use small groups of 10 to 15 persons selected to represent a complete vertical segment of the organization or department (vertical sensing), or a horizontal slice (horizontal sensing). The persons in horizontal sensing groups may be executives, middle managers, professionals, support staff, or frontline workers, but only one or two levels are included in each group.

A similar method used by marketing researchers is the *focus group* (Calder, 1977). Focus groups give participants the opportunity to discuss their needs. At the same time, they give focus group leaders the chance to ask questions and obtain detailed information about the attitudes and beliefs of participants. Focus groups are small, usually involving 6 to 10 participants who represent the population or subgroup being studied. The internal evaluator facilitates group interaction and the free exchange of ideas. Because the opinions of one participant affect the opinions of the other group members, focus group findings typically are verified against data from other sources, such as telephone surveys or key informant interviews.

Example: A communitywide needs assessment of the training needs of employment-disadvantaged groups included separate focus groups with (a) community service agencies, (b) potential employers, and (c) potential clients. Representatives from the service agencies and employers received a verbal and a written personal invitation, a list of questions that would be discussed, and a list of the other organizations invited to attend. Potential clients were contacted through advertisements in newspapers and on local cable television, through community agencies, and by flyers. The focus groups were co-led by an internal evaluator and a program staff person, and they lasted about 90 minutes.

Community Group Techniques

Community agencies and education systems in the United States, Canada, and in several other countries conduct needs assessments as part of their long-range planning process and to validate their needs and set priorities. Community group techniques supplement survey and indicator analysis methods by providing a current community perspective about the data (McKillip, 1987). Community group methods enhance the reliability of judgments concerning the priority of needs in the community. Versions of these techniques have found widespread use in business, industrial, and governmental organizations.

Community forums. A community forum is a rapid and economical way to elicit the insights of community residents concerning the accessibility, availability, and adequacy of services. A community forum is a meeting between two and four hours long giving all community residents the chance to discuss a specific issue, such as the need for particular services. It provides a way to reach persons underrepresented in census and utilization studies. Because the credibility of the community forum depends on the range of community representation, effective advertising to attract the right mix of people is essential. More than one type of media should be used (e.g., flyers, community cable TV ads), and careful consideration should be given to attracting hard-to-reach groups (e.g., ethnic groups, people living in high-rise developments, high-risk populations). Refreshments, prize drawings, free babysitting, transportation, a brief movie, and similar incentives may be used to make the forum compete successfully for people's time.

Community forums are community events that are orchestrated in consultation with community leaders, led by a respected member of the community, and held in a convenient community location. Given that the principal drawback of a community forum is the short time available for all persons to speak, the internal evaluator should plan procedures that enable participants to voice their opinions without monopolizing the discussion. For example, each speaker may be limited to a maximum "airtime" of two minutes per question. After the forum, the internal evaluator integrates the community forum data with other needs assessment data and provides rapid feedback about the results to the organization's managers.

Nominal group and Delphi techniques. The nominal group technique avoids the unstructured interaction style of the community forum in favor of a disciplined interplay between individual work and group interaction (Delbecq, Van de Ven, & Gustafson, 1975). The main advantage of the nominal group technique is that it allows time for generating ideas and protects each individual from competitive group pressures or domination by any one point of view. The Delphi technique provides a systematic procedure for collecting and organizing the views of informed persons while protecting dissenting or unusual opinions. The hallmark of the Delphi technique is the use of anonymous questionnaires and sequenced feedback to arrive at a group consensus. Carl Moore (1987) provides detailed guidelines for running nominal groups and using the Delphi method.

EVALUABILITY ASSESSMENT

Whereas a needs assessment helps organizations identify gaps and set priorities, an evaluability assessment verifies that the organization's programs are responding to the priority needs. An evaluability assessment also determines if a program's goals and objectives are congruent with the organization's mission and if they are measurable. As a tool for systematic internal evaluation, evaluability assessment provides a concise description of the organization's programs and how each one relates to the whole.

Evaluability assessment is usually a detailed procedure that takes six months or more to accomplish (see Rutman, 1980; Schmidt, Scanlon, & Bell, 1979; Wholey, 1979). Internal evaluators usually have weeks rather than months to complete an evaluability assessment. Faced with severe time strictures, internal evaluators may require an abbreviated procedure instead of the full one (Love & Hagarty, 1985). The managers and internal evaluators draft a set of three models for each program. The first model is a logic model that describes in diagram form the assumptions, sequence of causal events, and expected outcomes of each project. The second type of model is a function model that provides a concise graphical description of the program activities that parallel each component of the program's logic model. Finally, a measurement model defines the measures and comparisons that will indicate the major project implementation milestones, program activities, and program outcomes. These are matched to each component of the logic and function models. Figure 4.1 provides an example of an integrated model of an employee assistance program.

The internal evaluators present the program profiles and models to senior managers and selected program staff. If the programs are evaluable, the internal evaluators facilitate the selection of measures and comparisons. If the programs are not evaluable, the internal evaluators help draft action plans for making the necessary changes. Once the changes are made, the internal evaluators revise the models, present the revised models, and facilitate the selection of measures and comparisons.

PROGRAM MONITORING

Once a program is implemented, program monitoring provides a systematic way of informing managers whether (a) a program is operating as planned (program *process*) and (b) it is reaching its intended participants (program *coverage*). According to the Evaluation Research Society Standards Committee (1982), program monitoring is "the least acknowledged but probably the most practiced category of evaluation, putting to rest the notion that the evaluator comes in, does the job and then leaves." (p. 10). The committee observed that organizations from the U.S. General Accounting Office (GAO) to human service agencies in states and provinces to military training facilities are required to monitor their programs.

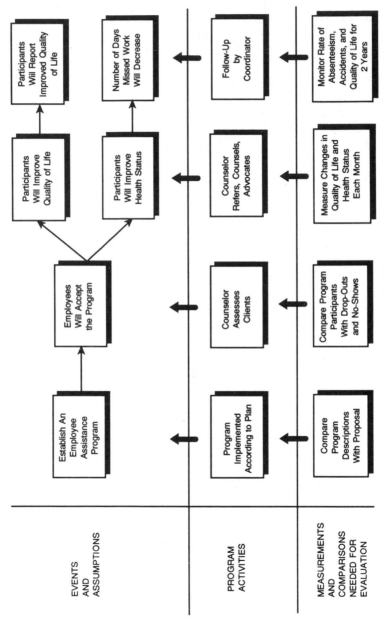

Figure 4.1. Integration of Logic, Function, and Measurement Models

To understand the value of monitoring information for managers, consider two of the manager's central uses of information: (a) to identify problems and opportunities, and (b) to build conceptual models. Monitoring information enables the manager to step back from the continual pressures and details of the manager's roles to see the broad picture. When potential problems or opportunities are identified, the manager can use the internal evaluator's time and analytic skills to investigate complex issues and develop models to help make choices and contingency plans.

The first steps in developing a monitoring system are familiar ones. The internal evaluator clarifies the information needs of the potential users and then works with them to select carefully and define the needed data. An important point to remember is that the information needs of the CEO, middle manager, and line manager are different. Internal evaluators are usually responsible for implementing the information systems and specialized techniques required for monitoring programs (Grant, 1978).

The capacity for systematic monitoring is the hallmark of a high quality monitoring system. A pitfall is confusing systematic with continuous monitoring. Systematic monitoring provides the requested information at the correct time, usually at specified periods, in a form easily understood by the manager. For example, the Discrepancy Evaluation Model (DEM) is widely used in special education programs and is one of the few internal evaluation models that emphasizes process activities, making it useful in monitoring program operations and compliance with state and federal laws (Hill & Hill, 1983). Continuous monitoring, on the other hand, may make sense for a computer-controlled assembly line, but the human manager will be overwhelmed by the volume of information.

The discipline for the internal evaluator is understanding the manager's information needs well enough so that the system provides only the minimum amount of information needed for monitoring. Monitoring information usually includes simple "turnstile statistics" (e.g., how many admissions or enrollments, dropouts, and no-shows), units of services delivered or products produced, outcomes of service, staff performance indicators (e.g., hours of direct and indirect services), costs, and revenues.

Although data for monitoring purposes may be obtained from interviews, direct observations, and questionnaire surveys, most of the time they must be extracted from management information systems. Management information systems collect data routinely to help manage the organization and its programs. These data are a valuable but neglected source of information for internal evaluations (Burstein, 1984; Chelimsky, 1985). A carefully designed management information system can provide reliable and inexpensive information for evaluations. Errol Porter (1989) provides an example of how he used existing data bases in conjunction with a comprehensive evaluation of the Employment Support Initiatives Program.

Example: All clients who entered the program during its first year of operation and a random-sample comparison group were tracked through computer tapes that included demographic data (e.g., age, education, location) and quarterly time-series data (e.g., type and amount of social assistance, amount earned from part-time jobs). The computer tapes provided large sample sizes and small sampling errors because almost all clients were tracked through the system. This stands in contrast to only 43% of the sample of program clients and 57% of the comparison group who were tracked in the client telephone survey. The computer tape data were used to validate the client telephone survey and assess the long-term impact of the program. The evaluators also formed longitudinal records of the individual clients, permitting accurate measures of their leaving the program and their recidivism.

Monitoring methods are a good way to start developing a program evaluation capability by providing the type of information system needed for successful evaluation. By keeping the information system simple and by making use of inexpensive microcomputer technology, internal evaluators can provide managers with the kind of information they need for systematic monitoring of the entire organization. Much of this same information may be used for planning, advocacy, and accountability purposes. Monitoring methods have limited ability to differentiate the impact of a program from effects caused by other events. They help the manager, however, to identify areas that require in-depth analysis. The following sections will describe four practical program monitoring methods that may be used by most organizations: program utilization studies, client satisfaction studies, quality assurance activities, and self-study.

PROGRAM UTILIZATION STUDIES

Program utilization or "pattern of use" studies are basically detailed descriptions of who uses the programs or services of an organization.

Program utilization studies, whether simple or sophisticated, are a key tool for internal evaluation (Landsberg, 1983). Pattern of use studies enable senior managers to offset the nearly exclusive emphasis funding bodies and boards of directors place on goal attainment. For example, if managers decide to provide services to a new group of clients, program utilization data is crucial in demonstrating that the new clients fit within the organization's values and mission statement, even if the services were not planned. Lack of ongoing program utilization data, on the other hand, can place managers in a highly vulnerable position if they decide to respond to an unforeseen need. Bocialetti and Kaplan (1986) illustrate this type of situation with the following example of an information and referral source funded by a major community foundation.

Example: In its 2-year evaluation, it was learned that the agency's referrals had steadily diminished and that it was providing direct services to clients (an unauthorized activity). The service was evaluated negatively while important data were ignored. The reason the service referrals had declined and direct services had increased was that the program operators found there were insufficient or totally lacking services to which to refer clients! As a result, they began providing those services themselves. This important information never reached the foundation through the [external] evaluation channels. (p. 3)

A basic form of pattern of use analysis gathers together demographic data about customers or clients (e.g., age, gender, place of residence), services used, and referral sources. The overall sample is then divided into subgroups based on the demographic categories. Next, utilization rates may be calculated based on the number of persons served per 1,000 residents in the capture (geographic) area. These are useful particularly for health, education, and social service programs.

This information may be compared with the demographic characteristics of the capture area population and with existing standards of need for specific types of services. These analyses give a quick indication of the availability, accessibility, and acceptability of a program. Subsequent analyses can provide answers to questions such as: Who are the referral sources? Is the program being used by the intended target groups? Are outreach efforts effective? Who are the heavy users of the program? Are certain types of persons finding the program inaccessible? What happens to participants after they leave the program?

Pattern of use studies are valuable tools for internal evaluation, and they are indispensable for public and voluntary sector organizations. If care is taken to analyze data in terms that are meaningful to funding bodies, utilization statistics represent a powerful bulwark against budget erosion. It is not difficult to argue, for example, that a heavily used service or a service used by a high-risk population is meeting a community need and should be funded at the same or a greater level.

The pattern of use study becomes more powerful when utilization data are compared with data from similar organizations. The major disadvantage of this approach to needs assessment is the assumption that the use and demand for services is the same as the need in the overall community. Other methods, such as community surveys and community forums, are more appropriate for assessing the needs of persons not currently using services.

Tracking the pattern of use over time permits internal evaluators to study factors that affect the movement of clients or customers through the organization's systems. This method was used by Bass and Windle (1972) to monitor a cohort (group) of clients as they moved through successive components of an agency's services. In this important work, longitudinal pattern of use studies enabled Bass and Windle to measure continuity of care by analyzing the effects such as different referral sources, intake procedures, waiting periods, preparation for treatment, and client acceptance of treatment. Although continuity of care has direct relevance to health and social service programs, the concept is applicable to virtually any program or organization where the consumer progresses through a series of services, for example, certain types of training, recreation, and government programs. A variation of this technique is the tracking of dropouts over time to uncover better ways of delivering services. Future demand for services may be projected by analyzing changes in trends measured by variables such as the number and type of referrals, severity of presenting problems, and length of service.

CLIENT SATISFACTION STUDIES

Client satisfaction studies (more recently known as *acceptance studies*) assist the organization in achieving its goals by anticipating consumer needs and providing services or products to meet those needs. The astonishing success of offshore industries, the privatization of public services, and competition for the donated dollar and the volunteer's time have made organizations in every sector of society keenly aware of the importance of understanding consumer needs. The internal evaluator occupies a pivotal position in helping today's organizations move from a product or service orientation to a consumer orientation in their bid to keep or increase their market share.

Managers must have accurate information about consumer response to their services and products. The drawback with consumer satisfaction studies has been their lack of precision. Consumer satisfaction scales tend to measure overall satisfaction (Larsen, Attkisson, Hargreaves, & Nguyen, 1979), and consumers completing the questionnaires are more likely to be the satisfied consumers. Consumers also feel pressure to give a positive response, and the finding that over 70% of consumers are satisfied with a service is typical.

With these limitations, why do internal evaluators conduct consumer satisfaction studies at all? It is a truism that techniques can be used to compensate for the bias in these methods, but there is no technique that can substitute for the perspectives given by direct consumer involvement in evaluation. Moreover, the value of consumer satisfaction studies comes as much from the process of involving consumers as from the results.

As general measures of satisfaction, these scales tap three important dimensions: (a) the extent to which the service or product has met the consumer's perceived needs; (b) overall consumer satisfaction with the service or product; and (c) whether the consumer would use the service or product again. Even general measures become useful tools when the data are collected systematically from consumers and norms are developed that permit comparisons among services or products.

As part of the internal evaluation process, consumer ratings lend themselves well to routine monitoring. Data collection methods include mail questionnaires and face-to-face or telephone interviews. Consumer ratings may be obtained at different times, such as after receiving the service or as part of a follow-up interview. The internal evaluator can reduce response bias and increase the benefits of consumer satisfaction studies in several ways. First, clients of certain types of organizations (e.g., health, mental health, social service) may be required to give their informed consent to participating in any study. This is an important opportunity to inform clients why the organization wants their feedback and to provide the desired response set by ensuring the confidentiality of their responses and that affirming accurate and candid feedback is desired.

Second, in situations where this initial contact isn't possible, many of the same benefits may be achieved by including the same messages in a letter from the CEO or department head together with a mailed questionnaire, or prior to a telephone interview.

Third, the internal evaluator is in a good position to obtain the major goals of the service or the name of the specific product from existing data bases (e.g., client records, product registrations). For example, the consumer can be asked to rate the achievement of the specific service goal, adding precision and personalizing the scale. Fourth, the internal evaluator also has a knowledge of what organizational events (e.g., turnover in staff, production line problems) are likely to influence satisfaction, and changes in these conditions can be used as control variables. Fifth, clients should be given frequent opportunities to express dissatisfactions and to give recommendations for change. Finally, consumer satisfaction methods are most useful when they are paired with other measures and collected consistently over time and across programs.

Example: During the course of the first phase of the Employment Support Initiatives (ESI) evaluation, clients were interviewed regarding their participation in the programs and their assessment of the programs' particular benefits and helpfulness (Love & Hagarty, 1985). Very few clients refused to be interviewed when contacted. This survey was used to evaluate program processes and outcomes, as well as to encourage client participation in the evaluation effort by providing a confidential channel for client feedback.

QUALITY ASSURANCE

Improved quality control in manufacturing and service industries has been called the greatest advance in the last decade. The concept of quality control is not new, but for over a quarter of a century quality control mechanisms were largely technical and statistical. Quality control consisted of methods of measuring deviations from an established standard of quality by taking samples of goods and services (acceptance sampling) and recording the results on charts. Statistical probability theory was applied to the sample results, trends and defects were spotted (process control), and corrective actions were taken. Internal evaluators organized and supervised quality control efforts. They worked with marketing and production staff to set standards of quality, devised methods for collecting data, trained inspectors, analyzed data, and provided feedback to managers in an effort to find the optimum quality of design.

More recently, quality *assurance* rather than quality control has emerged as a key concept. Quality assurance is seen as a pervasive attitude coupled with methods of managing and motivating people. The widespread popularity of the concept of excellence, promoted by Thomas J. Peters (Peters & Austin, 1986; Peters & Waterman, 1982), has contributed to the acceptance of quality assurance methods. The historical roots of quality assurance procedures, however, are evidenced in the four principles that form the basis of Crosby's (1979, 1985) theory of quality management: definition, system, performance standard, and measurement. Although quality is still defined as adherence to measurable standards, it is not measured after the service or good has been produced. Quality is managed by establishing systems that prevent defects from occurring in the first place. Performance standards are established by defining the job requirements and explaining them to each worker verbally. Crosby argues that this process produces zero defects. If a defect appears, then a team of managers and workers discovers what went wrong and takes corrective action.

The small collaborative team of managers and workers meeting regularly to solve problems and implement solutions is called a quality circle (Lawler & Mohrman, 1985; Mohr & Mohr, 1983). This method is the backbone of modern quality assurance approaches in both manufacturing and service organizations. Quality circles are a form of organizational self-evaluation. Because quality circles are data-based interventions, internal evaluators usually have the job of training managers and employees in quality control methods, quality measurement, and interpersonal techniques.

What if quality circles and other quality assurance techniques fail to prevent poor quality? Usually, persistent problems can be traced to fundamental flaws in the process of service delivery or production of goods. In these situations, internal evaluators can bring rapid improvements through a process study. Within the quality assurance context, a process study involves a systematic investigation of the existing or proposed methods.

This is a modern form of the work study, work simplification, and job design aspects of production engineering (Mogensen, 1963; Rowland, 1984). Like quality circles, it involves the participation of workers, managers, and support staff in small study teams. The first step is verifying that the correct method is being implemented in all locations. Sometimes incorrect implementation in one site produces misleading results. The second step is examining the reports of poor quality in search of obvious flaws in the method. If this fails, evaluation studies are undertaken. These may include describing in detail the method of service delivery or production, diagramming the structure and sequence of events used in the method, developing guidelines for an improved method, training personnel in the new process, and implementing and monitoring the new method.

Quality assurance is based on the assumptions that quality can be measured and that reliable methods of measurement are available. Many types of goods and services do not permit the measurement of quality. The presence or absence of a defect is the key factor. For example, in a community service agency, the presence or absence of a mandatory assessment report is noted. Facts such as these cannot be measured, but they can be counted. These quality assurance techniques are not so precise, but they provide a practical solution in situations where measurements are not feasible.

SELF-STUDY

Managers in the 1990s are being influenced strongly by a set of social values that promote democratic participation, trust, responsibility, and accountability. This has translated into management philosophies that stress local accountability for program results, program quality, financial management, and organizational effectiveness. Local accountability, however, does not occur by magic: It requires organizational structures, evaluation tools, and reporting mechanisms to satisfy local managers and their masters that the intended results are being achieved. Self-study is becoming an increasingly popular and important evaluation tool to show these mechanisms are in place.

Self-study is the process of using an organization's own staff to monitor its performance systematically against established standards. The most comprehensive use of self-study is as part of an *accreditation* review. Accreditation is a process of certification that was developed originally for professions and health facilities (e.g., Joint Commission on the Accreditation of Hospitals, Canadian Council on Hospital Accreditation) but now has been adopted in a wide variety of educational and human service settings (e.g., Council on Accreditation, Commission on Accreditation of Rehabilitation Facilities). The self-study provides a snapshot of how well an organization (a) meets mandatory federal, state/provincial, and municipal requirements; (b) establishes methods of program delivery that meet high professional standards; (c) monitors the quality of its goods and services; (d) employs qualified and experienced staff and provides adequate supervision; (e) develops an organizational structure that enables effective management; (f) achieves its intended results; and (g) maintains financial and personnel systems that permit efficient and responsible use of the organization's resources.

There are four key ingredients in the self-study process:

- setting of recognized standards;
- rating the standards;
- making any changes necessary to meet the standards; and
- confirming the achievement of the standards by external evaluators.

In the case of an accreditation self-study, the standards are set by an accrediting body after extensive consultation with experts in the field, including professional staff, managers, and members of boards. The standards reflect a broad consensus of the knowledge and experience of persons in the field of interest. These standards, and the rating scales for measuring their achievement, appear in a written self-study document. The self-study emphasizes the developmental and educational aspects of the evaluation process by providing a clear set of standards and sufficient time to allow changes before undergoing a formal review by external evaluators. The case example below illustrates the self-study process.

Example: A multiservice community health organization wants to be accredited. From the national accrediting body it receives a self-study manual that contains a list of several hundred standards and a rating scale for measuring their achievement. The standards cover every aspect of agency operation and management. Over the next few months, study teams meet independently and complete the ratings in their areas of expertise. The team leaders then assess the agency's strengths and weaknesses and formulate a work plan to correct deficiencies. When the organization is ready, the accrediting body sends an independent team of peer reviewers to check that the agency has achieved the required number of standards.

The case study illustrates the importance of forming work groups to evaluate the achievement of standards. This ensures participation in the self-study process and a commitment to achieving the desired results.

Other forms of self-study also emphasize the importance of the work group. For example, Newman, O'Reilly, and Van Wijk (1987) outline a process for self-evaluation and planning for human service organizations based on monitoring the achievement of major program and agency goals. According to their approach, the first step for successful self-evaluation is organizing a small work group of four to eight members representing all levels of the organization. In the field of education, Friedel and Papik (1986) describe the self-study process developed by the Eastern Iowa Community College District. Phase I involves a collection of program descriptive data through a self-study document that is completed by program/department faculty. This self-study document requests information about the curriculum, course development, the articulation agreement, equipment, facilities, the advisory committee, faculty, students, placement, and testing, in addition to a cost analysis of the program.

SUMMARY

Systematic internal evaluation begins when an organization analyzes its information needs and reaches common agreement on the content, categories, and systems for data collection and reporting. This permits the organization to monitor its operations and to help managers understand the organization's activities, thereby making the activities more manageable.

There is a variety of practical methods for systematic internal evaluation: needs assessment, program utilization studies, evaluability assessment, systematic program monitoring, consumer/client satisfaction studies, quality assurance, and self-study. *Needs assessment* reveals gaps between current results and desired outcomes and sets priorities among needs. *Evaluability assessment* documents the relationships among program components and appraises the readiness of the program to undergo rigorous evaluation of its impact.

Program monitoring arguably is the most practiced type of goal evaluation. Program monitoring supplies managers with regular feedback about program operations and early warnings of potential trouble. For internal evaluation, four practical approaches for program monitoring are program utilization studies, client satisfaction studies, quality assurance activities, and self-study. *Program utilization* studies describe who uses the programs or services of an organization. *Client satisfaction* studies provide information to managers about consumer acceptance and consumer satisfaction. *Quality assurance* studies evaluate the quality of a product or service as well as assess the methods used to monitor quality. Finally, *self-study* enables an organization to monitor its performance by having its staff rate the organization's attainment of recognized standards.

EXERCISES

Arrange a meeting with the manager and several staff to discuss the information they find useful in managing and operating the program. During this meeting:

1. Determine how the program assesses its needs. Describe the methods the program uses for needs assessment and write a brief summary of its major needs.
2. If needs assessments are not done, discuss the various methods described in this chapter with the manager and arrive at the method(s) that suit the program best.
3. Determine who the manager considers to be the key informants about the program or organization. What constituencies do they represent?
4. Does the manager employ (a) service utilization studies or (b) ongoing monitoring for evaluation or planning purposes? What performance indicators are tracked using these methods? Provide several examples of how they are used for decision making.
5. Meet with the program staff, and use the methods of evaluability assessment (a) to develop a logic model of the program that includes goals, program activities, and performance measures; and (b) to assess the staff and program readiness for evaluation.
6. What are staff attitudes toward conducting consumer/client satisfaction surveys? What questions do they consider worth asking?
7. What methods of quality assurance does the program use? What types of quality assurance methods are feasible for this program?

5

Evaluating Goal Achievement

Goal evaluation enables the organization to *compare* the actual achievement of goals with the intended achievement. Goal evaluation enables managers to answer the comparative question, "Is this what should be?" This is not the same thing as monitoring goal attainment, which is a descriptive (not a comparative) activity. Goal evaluation also is more than a set of measurement techniques. Goal evaluation requires the organizational structures for involving managers and staff in the process of defining potential goals, negotiating reasonable and measurable goals among constituent groups, assessing goal priorities, and designing the data collection and reporting systems. This chapter discusses the elements of goal evaluation, methods for defining goals, and ways of solving some of the persistent problems surrounding the evaluation of goals. Then it presents several methods of goal evaluation, including budgeting, management by objectives, goal monitoring, and goal attainment scaling.

THE ELEMENTS OF GOAL EVALUATION

A basic requirement of the goal evaluation process is setting standards for goal performance. These standards may be either quantitative ("Increase service by 15% during the next quarter") or qualitative ("Improve worker morale"). Next, it involves establishing information feedback mechanisms that report goal attainment. To ensure that the goals are achieved, these information systems must measure the attainment of goals and provide timely information to managers that enables corrective action to be taken. Finally, goal evaluation includes an analysis of goals and a diagnosis of problems in goal achievement over a period of time that is used to modify future plans.

Goals may be general or specific and may encompass time spans ranging from a few months to several years. Goals may be set for the entire organization, programs, or individuals. Goals at the various organizational levels must be coordinated if the organization is to achieve its intended purposes. This coordination is achieved by the direction and policies set by the board of an organization and by the activities of managers of departments and units. Finally, there must be coordination of the long-term goals of the organization with the short-term goals of departments and programs, and of both of these with the personal goals of workers.

PROBLEMS WITH EVALUATING GOALS

Why Evaluators Are Confused by Goals

In the field of evaluation, the concept of goals has caused considerable confusion and controversy. Part of the problem is that evaluators seem unaware that goal setting had its genesis in two different backgrounds: staff development and systems development. Just like internal evaluation, goal setting is both a planning and control system and a powerful method of behavioral change and organizational development. Adding to the confusion, the meaning of the term goal setting has cycled back and forth between these two traditions during the last 25 years.

The staff-development foundations of goal setting started earlier in this century when it was used as a tool for human resources management that was closely linked to reward systems. These methods shared historical roots with the time and motion studies and incentive systems developed for workers in manufacturing industries.

The systems-development foundations began when the essential nature of organizations was identified as teleological or goal seeking (Gibb, 1954; Simon, 1964). The primacy of organizational goals is reflected in modern definitions that see management as "a social and technical process that utilizes resources, influences human action, and facilitates changes in order to accomplish the organization's goals" (Haimann, Scott, & Connor, 1978, p. 9). Peter Drucker (1954) nurtured the systems-development foundations of goal setting when he coined the phrase "management by objectives" (MBO) and stressed that organizations must set goals in eight vital areas: productivity, market standing, innovation, physical and financial resources, profitability, manager performance and development, worker performance and attitude, and public responsibility. Odiorne (1965) operationalized the concept of MBO and emphasized the need for quantitative measurement.

The systems-development tradition emphasized the clarification of overall organizational goals, planning and control systems, and the mechanics of designing a management system. McGregor (1957) sparked a return to the earlier staff-development roots of goal setting as he struggled to reconcile the importance of MBO with its apparent limitations. It was well-known that some organizations had goals that were conflicting, ignored in favor of personal goals, or simply never achieved. McGregor felt MBO should ensure that both organizational and individual goals be identified and attained. He emphasized the qualitative aspects of MBO and its role in development. The original MBO technique was modified by having workers participate in the setting of their goals and the assessment of goal attainment.

As a participative management tool, MBO integrates the goals of the organization with those of managers and individual workers. Participation with workers in goal setting increases the manager's knowledge of the situation and improves the quality of decision making. Progress on goals may be monitored individually or by work groups.

By clarifying the duties and responsibilities of individuals or work groups, the developmental approach to MBO helps specify the types of organizational and personal outcomes required to achieve the desired results. Further, goal setting identifies the type of data needed to assess progress on goals and the managerial supports needed to achieve them. For their part, reward systems reinforce goal setting by rewarding people for achieving their goals. For example, at the work group or department level, goal setting can direct group action and reward overall group outcomes. At the individual job level, goal setting can shape the work of individuals and reward behaviors producing the desired performance outcomes.

As the field of evaluation was developing in the late 1960s and 1970s, virtual anarchy reigned concerning the terms *goals, goal setting,* and MBO and whether these methods were part of the planning, budgeting, performance appraisal, or compensation processes. Wickstrom (1968, p. 1) captured the state of affairs when he said: "Management by objectives has become an all purpose term, meaning almost anything one chooses it to mean."

GOAL DEFINITION

Organizations are generally expected to meet certain needs or solve particular problems. To focus their efforts, organizations usually plan their activities and define them using the language of goals. It follows, therefore, that the fundamental way to measure the results of organizations is to measure the achievement of goals. This conclusion is logical only if the goal formulation process really works. Although it is assumed that planners and managers have paid attention to goal definition, it is rare to find situations where it has been properly undertaken (see Table 5.1). Instead it is common to find goals that are vaguely stated in global terms, contradictory goals, or goals unrelated to the program's activities. In addition, there may be implicit goals that the program pursues but that are not formally stated. This leads to the inability to judge goal achievement.

Planners, managers, and evaluators can benefit from the process of goal definition. Goals provide a basis for determining what particular aspects of an overall problem are given priority. Goals reflect the accepted diagnosis or causal explanation, help identify the philosophical foundation of the program, and recognize conflicting and competing goals. Moreover, clearly specifiable goals provide the basis for holding programs accountable. Because goals serve as the criteria of the program's success, they must be clearly specified for the purpose of developing measures. If goal definition has not been handled adequately through the planning and management process, then the internal evaluator must undertake the process of goal definition. The process of goal definition provides some assurance that crucial variables have been identified that will be included in the evaluation. The failure to go through this process presents a potential danger of not including important variables in the evaluation simply because there was no effort to identify program goals properly.

The aim of the goal definition process is a clear and specific statement of what the organization or program expects to be achieved in a given area. In other words, it is a statement of observable effects that are expected from a set of actions. Examples of good goal statements are the administrative goal "to reduce accidents by 4%," the sales goal, "to maintain gross sales margins for Bea's Bonnets at 40%," or the service goal "to deliver 10 new adolescent recreation programs by December 1st." Each of these goals is specific, the outcomes are clear, and an objective observer could verify if the goals were achieved or not.

In these examples, the goals are linked to criteria or indicators that show the goal has been reached. Indicators also may be used to measure the rate of goal attainment or how well the goal was attained. During

Table 5.1

Methodological Problems of Goal Evaluation:
Latent Goals and Unintended Effects

• *Identifying Key Goals.* The major problem goal is only one goal of a program and there are other important goals concerned with survival and growth (e.g., obtaining resources, coordination, response to pressures). The evaluation ignores these secondary goals.

• *Clarifying Goals.* There is difficulty identifying "real" goals from those that represent political rhetoric, provide justification for funding requests, mobilize support, and legitimize the program.

• *Changing Goals.* Goals are always changing, either because the mandate allows goal modification, or because there is adaptation and change.

• *Ignoring Unintended Effects.* The emphasis on clearly defined goals means that unanticipated side effects are ignored.

The exclusive focus on formally stated goals is inadequate. The task of the internal evaluator is to identify latent goals as well as anticipated effects (either intended or unintended) by recognizing the claims of various parties who have stated the program will produce a particular positive or negative effect.

---

the goal definition process the indicators are set at the level of intended results (e.g., "10 new adolescent recreation programs"). This is called the expected level. The success in reaching a goal may be measured in terms of the expected level; this process forms the basis of simple goal evaluation methods as well as more complex methodology, such as goal attainment scaling.

Although quantitative indicators are preferable, the internal evaluator should carefully avoid the "measurement trap." Important goals in key result areas should be set whether or not they are easily measurable. Often measures are not readily apparent, but the standards can be developed over time. Nothing is more demoralizing for a planning group than debating goal indicators or trying to set goal priorities and develop measures at the same time. At best, it can lead to setting poor indicators; at worst, it can lead to selecting trivial goals with indicators that are easily measured. One way around this dilemma is to break the meeting into three parts: first, a goal-setting session, then a homework session to draft indicators, and finally a meeting to review goals and indicators.

MANAGEMENT BY OBJECTIVES (MBO)

Based on their work at General Electric, Huse and Kay (1964) developed practical guidelines for implementing goal setting and MBO in organizations. MBO is an iterative, cyclical approach based on three psychological principles (Huse, 1966):

- *Knowledge of Expectations.* MBO can reduce role ambiguity and role conflict by clarifying expectations for both managers and workers.
- *Knowledge of Results.* MBO can improve job performance by providing individualized, timely, and supportive feedback about the achievement of specific results.
- *Coaching and Counseling.* MBO can improve learning by providing appropriate coaching and counseling to solve problems identified through a process of open discussion.

Negative consequences have resulted primarily from concentrating on the organizational and measurement aspects of goal setting and MBO. Setting goals based on organizational goals without considering personal and career goals causes coordination and communication problems by eliminating mutual problem solving. Likewise, overemphasis on quantitative measures can lead to the pursuit of measurable but less important goals, while key goals are ignored.

Example: By measuring performance on the basis of money and supplies received from donors, the staff of an international disaster relief organization neglected getting the supplies quickly to persons in need and constructing temporary shelters.

The concern with measures makes goal setting appear as a reward-punishment system that weakens teamwork among managers. Research has shown that improvements are produced only when managers and workers agree on mutually acceptable specific goals and measures of both intangible and tangible results. This works well in a participative culture that permits using information for self-evaluation and self-management.

Goal setting and MBO have increased the level of productivity whether they are set unilaterally by managers or jointly by managers and workers (Latham & Locke, 1979). Attempts to install goal setting and MBO in an exploitative-authoritative organizational culture, however, usually results in resistance to the perceived manipulation and increased reporting demands of the system.

BUDGETING

Using Budgets for Internal Evaluation

For many organizations, budgets are the primary method of goal evaluation. Budgets provide information about the performance of the organization. By comparing actual and budgeted results and costs, differences or variances can be identified and studied. By reporting exceptions only, budgets can be used as a convenient method of diagnosis and control. Managers can then analyze the reasons for the variances and take the necessary corrective actions. Budgets are a powerful management tool because performance can be related to the responsible managers and because budget controls permit managers to work together within clearly defined policies and guidelines.

Budgeting is the setting of quantitative performance goals for the future. Budgets may set financial goals, such as revenues or capital costs, or other numerical goals, such as units of service or numbers of sales. Budgets provide a clear way of setting goals and coordinating the organization's activities. The budget captures the authorized plan for spending, and the accounting system reports the actual amounts spent. In devising budgets, forecasts are made and there is an assessment of constraints and opportunities. First, budgets for each area of functional responsibility (e.g., marketing, production) are developed. Next, budgets are drawn up for each department and included within the functional budgets. Areas should reflect the responsibility of managers, and also are called budget or cost centers. Finally, the functional budgets are integrated into a total budget.

Using budgets for goal evaluation requires a good accounting system. A good accounting system has two essential features. First, the information reported should be accurate and reliable. This demands using a double-entry system, in which debits equal credits. Some public and nonprofit organizations still use single-entry systems, but the information generated by these systems is not reliable enough for evaluation purposes. Second, accounts should match each item on the budget. This situation often occurs when an organization switches to a program budget, but it does not convert the accounting system. Reconciling the two systems through crosswalking is possible, but the level of accuracy is less than required for evaluation.

The straightforward approach for using budgets to evaluate goals is combining program budget data with performance measurement information. In contrast to a *line-item budget,* which focuses on expense components (e.g., salaries, fringe benefits, supplies), the *program budget* concentrates on programs and program components (e.g., training, program activities, administration). Performance measurement information defines the *planned outputs,* which may include *workload* measures and *results* measures. For example, in a school setting, the budget defined the workload in terms of expected enrollments and student-teacher ratios, and the results in terms of student achievement scores and the number of students graduated. Chapter 7 explains these concepts at length in the discussion of the evaluation of efficiency goals.

GOAL MONITORING

Not only are organizations goal-seeking systems, they are information-processing systems as well. Regular information about the achievement of major organizational and program goals is an essential component of internal evaluation. Sometimes this regular monitoring of goals is called performance measurement or outcome monitoring. Goal evaluation information can have a positive impact on goal attainment if managers and workers use it correctly.

Information feedback helps to clarify goals and to motivate performance, solve problems, and correct deviations from planned directions. Depending on the nature of the goals that have been set, information can be supplied to an individual manager or an entire department. Feedback can report the quantity or quality of goal performance, or it can provide information about the programs or processes. Goal evaluation requires a careful consideration of information systems, because they are essential to spotlight key goals and provide feedback about goal achievement.

Internal evaluation is more than a set of techniques: It is a powerful organizational *intervention.* Poorly designed information feedback systems can be dangerous because they focus attention on unimportant goals. First, managers and internal evaluators must have a clear picture of the entire organization and the relationship of different types of goals to each other. For example, in an effort to control costs, a community service organization closely monitored the amount of materials used by workers, but virtually no information was kept about direct service time or units of service. Yet nearly 50% of client appointments were missed, and salary costs represented 80% of the agency's budget.

Second, not only must information feedback systems focus on the right goals, they must use the right measures. Peter Drucker (1954) wrote, "the measurement used determines what one pays attention to. It makes things visible and tangible. The things included in the management become relevant; the things omitted are out of sight and out of mind" (p. 64). Goal measurement includes measurement of tangibles (e.g., "to increase production of Magic Marvels by 2%") and intangibles (e.g., "to improve morale in the Devil's Dungeon branch plant").

Third, the process of feedback is important. The type of feedback, how often it is reported, and how it is used are crucial. Planning information feedback starts with the needs of the users. For goal evaluation, users may include multiple audiences, such as the board and CEO, middle and line managers, and workers. The information reported should help users identify actual results compared with intended results, plan better goals, and select among alternate courses of action.

Fourth, information about the achievement of organizational goals should be integrated with information about the attainment of managers' and workers' personal goals.

For internal evaluation, the "on-going feedback system" (Nadler, Mirvis, & Cammann, 1976) provides a useful goal evaluation model that is compatible with goal setting and MBO principles. This system offers several major features: Feedback measures are designed and reviewed by the information users themselves; managers and workers participate in the design process; feedback about goals and organizational processes is included; feedback is given to users at all levels in the organization; managers are trained in the use of feedback information; and systems implementation is carefully designed. Nadler et al. (1976) describe the following example of an information feedback system implementation.

Example: The staff of a large bank in a midwestern city wanted to improve the functioning of their 20-branch retail banking system. A task force designed a feedback system that included branch performance in the areas of loans and tellers and overall branch performance in terms of employee behavior (absenteeism, turnover), employee effectiveness (quality of customer service), and financial achievement (profitability). An attitudinal scale measured the organizational process in each branch.

GOAL ATTAINMENT SCALING

Goal attainment scaling (GAS) was devised as a general method for process and outcome evaluation of services provided to individual clients as well as by entire programs (Kiresuk, 1973; Kiresuk & Lund, 1975; Kiresuk & Sherman, 1968). Other methods of goal evaluation (e.g., MBO, goal monitoring), measured simply whether a goal was attained or not. The GAS method modified the rating of goal attainment to include degrees of goal attainment.

Goal attainment scaling was devised as a flexible tool for internal evaluation. For example, GAS served as the basis of the internal evaluation system at Hennepin County Mental Health Service (Kiresuk & Lund, 1975) and at other organizations for both summative and formative internal evaluations of organizational goals. In this context, *summative evaluation* means rating goals once to evaluate the overall impact of the program, and *formative evaluation* means assessing goals periodically and using the information for program improvement.

The technique held sufficient promise in the 1970s as a universal evaluation method that a program evaluation resource center was established to develop and promote goal attainment scaling. Concerns about using individualized client goals rather than the same measuring instrument for all clients, the validity of the scales, and using GAS to compare programs moved GAS from the center stage of evaluation strategies (Calsyn & Davidson, 1978; Smith & Cardillo, 1979). When used with other measures, GAS still finds a useful place among the goal evaluation methods of internal evaluators. GAS permits a convenient way to monitor the attainment of intermediate goals on a monthly basis and then aggregate them into an overall performance index (Bolin & Kivens, 1975). By involving staff and clients in the goal-setting process, GAS appears to improve morale, motivate staff to achieve goals, and provide corrective feedback (Stelmachers, Lund, & Meade, 1972). Fiester (1978) presents an example of the use of a simplified form of GAS as part of an internal evaluation system in a children's mental health center.

Example: Parents received an assessment instrument listing 100 child prob-lem behaviors, which were organized into 14 preset categories. The internal evaluators organized goals into the same 14 preset "skill areas," which helped standardize the goals. Shortly after treatment began the therapist and client, using the completed assessment instrument, established up to a maximum of three goals. At the end of treatment, therapists rated goal attainment. The internal evaluators then contacted clients and/or key informants by telephone and had them rate goal attainment and client satisfaction.

SUMMARY

Setting goals is a fundamental way of achieving high performance. Goal setting is a complex process. Optimal performance requires the careful coordination of personal and organizational goals at all manage-ment levels. Evaluating goals, in turn, entails the setting of standards for goal achievement and then measuring the attainment of those stan-dards. Goal evaluation usually includes a diagnosis of problems in goal achievement over a period of time.

The method of *goal definition* ensures that goals are specific and measurable. For many organizations, *budgeting* provides the way of setting financial and other numerical goals (e.g., number of sales, units of service) and coordinating the organization's activities. Some organi-zations use *management by objectives* (MBO) as a way of setting and measuring goals following a yearly planning and budgeting cycle. For the majority of organizations, *goal monitoring* is a simple method that supplies managers and boards with the information essential for man-agement planning and control. In many human service organizations, a form of *goal attainment scaling* (GAS) provides a useful way of mea-suring client progress and outcomes.

EXERCISES

Choose one of the following three areas for an assignment:

1. *Goal Evaluation.* Interview the manager and at least one staff person. Ask them the questions below. Then obtain a written description of the goals of the program. Compare the interview data with the written descriptions in a brief written report.

(a) What are the mission and major goals of the overall organization?

(b) What are the major goals for the program? Are the goals outcome goals (i.e., results expected) or are they process goals (i.e., efforts delivered)?

(c) What are the indicators of program goal attainment? Are they measurable?

(d) How often are the program goals evaluated? Who participates in the evaluation? What evidence is used?

(e) What are the individual goals of the manager and staff person?

(f) How do the individual goals relate to the program and organizational goals?

(g) What are the indicators of individual goal attainment? Are they measurable?

(h) How often are the individual goals evaluated? Who participates in the evaluation?

(i) What conclusions do you draw about the usefulness of goals at levels of the organization, the program, and the individual?

2. *Budgets.* Interview the manager and the financial officer about the budgeting process. Compare their answers in a written report.

(a) What is the annual budget cycle for the program? The organization?

(b) Describe the fit between the budgeting cycle and the planning cycle.

(c) How does the program budget fit with program and organizational goals?

(d) Are budgets used to evaluate programs? How?

(e) What are the problems the manager and the financial officer experience with using budgets for internal evaluation?

3. *Information Feedback.* Interview a senior manager and a line manager (or supervisor) and compare their answers to the following questions in a brief report.

(a) What type of information feedback do they consider essential to manage their work well?

(b) What type of information feedback do they actually receive?

(c) What effect does the information feedback have on them? On their performance?

(d) Is the information feedback reviewed by workers?

(e) What is the workers' response to this information? Does it change the way they do their jobs? How?

6

Effectiveness Evaluation

WHAT IS EFFECTIVENESS?

In his book *The Functions of the Executive*, Chester Barnard (1938) first differentiated between two of these dimensions, using the terms *effectiveness* and *efficiency*, and his definitions are still used today. Both effectiveness and efficiency measure *outputs*, that is, the products, services, and other items (e.g., regulations, tax law provisions) directly produced by a program or organization. *Effectiveness* refers to the degree of correspondence between the actual outputs of a system and the desired outputs. *Efficiency* means the ratio of actual outputs to actual inputs (e.g., money, staff, skills) of the program or organization.

In simpler terms, Peter Drucker (1954, 1974) said effectiveness is doing the right things, and efficiency is doing things right. Effectiveness concentrates on results, and efficiency on the process used to obtain those results. Effectiveness and efficiency are two measures of output, and they are both crucial measures of performance. Even the most efficient organization cannot survive if it is efficient at doing the wrong things. Likewise, the organization with the greatest effectiveness can disintegrate from poor efficiency. Nonetheless, the highest level of efficiency couldn't help the makers of buggy whips or steam locomotives prevail in the face of shifting demands.

This chapter discusses effectiveness; Chapter 7 discusses efficiency.

FORMULATING THE RIGHT QUESTIONS FOR EVALUATING EFFECTIVENESS

The failure to ask the *right* questions is a major reason for the lack of high-quality evaluations of program effectiveness. Right now there is considerable confusion about the range of questions that should be included in these evaluations. The typology of common evaluation questions created by Nick Smith (1987) provides a useful way of clarifying this situation. Smith states that the process of evaluation involves making justifiable claims about the object under study. A claim is essentially a question-answer proposition, that is, an answer to a question of interest. According to Smith, there are four common types of claims encountered in effectiveness evaluation: research claims, policy claims, evaluation claims, and management claims. Based on Smith's work, Table 6.1 lists the key questions associated with each type of claim.

The heart of the problem is that much of the work of professional evaluators has focused on *research* questions; management, policy, and evaluative questions have been to a large extent ignored. Research questions emphasize the role of *inquiry* in the evaluation process. Research claims seek to describe the general situation and explain its causes. They are answers to questions such as: What are the components of this program as implemented? Did this program cause the intended results better than a competing program? A major shortcoming on the part of managers, funders, consumers, and other stakeholders is assuming that demonstrating the effectiveness of a technique by answering research questions means that any program using the technique in another setting will also be effective (Flay & Best, 1982). A potent technique will not contribute to the effectiveness of a program unless the technique is delivered by competent staff to a clearly defined target group under favorable conditions (Sechrest, West, Phillips, Redner, & Yeaton, 1979; Yeaton & Redner, 1981).

In contrast, internal evaluation focuses primarily on management questions. These are practical questions with *action* claims. Ultimately managers need to decide and take action by answering the question: Should we do the program here? In making this decision they also need answers to other questions: Who wants the program? Can the program be done here? What are the costs of doing the program here? What are the benefits of doing the program here? Answers to management questions, therefore, depend on the *local situation,* and the answers will be different from organization to organization.

Policy questions are similar to management questions, except at a broader level. They are practical questions, and the answers are action claims. The primary question is: Which policies are good? Policy questions share with evaluative questions a concern about value claims. This requires answering questions concerning the political support for the program or policy, the overall value of the program or policy, the value of components of the program or policy, the best way of combining program or policy alternatives, and ways to make the program or policy better.

Table 6.1
Types of Effectiveness Claims Made in Evaluation and Their Corresponding Questions

Type of Claim	Questions
Management	What is the program?
	Who wants the program?
	Can the program be done here?
	What are the costs of doing the program here?
	What are the benefits of doing the program here?
	Should we do the program here?
Policy	What policy should the organization follow?
	What are the implications of this policy?
	Does this policy conflict with other policies?
	Is there political support for this policy?
	How do we implement this policy?
Evaluation	Is this a good program?
	How can this program be improved?
	Is this program better than a competing program?
Research	What is the definition of this type of program?
	What are the components of this program as implemented?
	What are the results of this program?
	Does this program cause the intended results?
	Does this program cause the intended results better than a competing program?

Evaluation questions are *value* claims. They ask about the worth or value of a program, often in comparison with a competing program. The key questions are: Is this a good program? How can this program be improved? Is this program better than a competing program? Scriven (1980) and Gowin (Novak & Gowin, 1984) provide further discussion of evaluation questions.

APPROACHES TO
EVALUATING EFFECTIVENESS

The most common motivation for studying effectiveness is to aid management and service providers in making a specific major decision about program change. Such studies deal with policy decisions about service delivery methods and are generally time-limited, rather than ongoing, monitoring activities.

A second approach, more closely linked to day-to-day management, is routine monitoring of performance to detect specific program strengths, weaknesses, or trouble spots. Only easily collected and inexpensive outcome indicators are practical, such as survival rates and symptom ratings at various stages of treatment, global ratings of functional impairment before and after receipt of services, and measures of client and consumer satisfaction. Normative data from the professional literature, or from funding and accreditation agencies, may be available for interpreting such measures. At the minimum, time trends within the same program and types of clients can be examined.

A third contribution of outcome evaluation to program management is to demonstrate whether each component of the program is functioning with reasonable effectiveness. It is difficult, given current technology and resources, to demonstrate overall program effectiveness. Untreated comparison groups are generally unavailable, and demonstrating program effectiveness requires normative studies among subsets of similar programs. The methods and resources for such studies are frequently lacking.

A fourth approach integrates costs of services with service outcomes and presents methods for cost-outcome and cost-effectiveness analyses. Sets of outcomes are specified and costs minimized for a given level of effectiveness.

Difficulty in using standardized outcome measures to assess quality and effectiveness of services arises from the diversity of vested interests. Satisfactory outcomes are defined in different ways by constituents. The search for realistic expectations and outcome norms is in its infancy. Program objectives may include other outcomes, such as community awareness of availability of services, community acceptance of service programs, or good staff morale.

It is useful to distinguish short-term outcomes that can be assessed easily during the course of providing service from long-range outcomes that may require data collection at some point following client exit from the service setting. Short-term outcomes represent a sensible starting place for examining many policy issues. The monitoring of these measures might be integrated into utilization review and client care audit procedures.

In the face of budget restraints, most organizations need to concentrate on the less costly ways of measuring effectiveness, such as ratings by frontline workers, self-administered instruments, available data, and simple mail and survey methods. This information is readily understood and more likely to be used. The data may already be available in the organization's records. Complex, extensive, or costly measures of client outcome are more appropriate for special projects than for ongoing internal evaluation and program oversight.

SELECTING A DESIGN

Evaluating program outcomes usually involves choosing an evaluation design strategy from two major types: (a) case study, and (b) group comparison designs. Although evaluative research emphasizes using group comparison designs, the choice of designs for internal evaluation studies depends on the type of questions asked, the type of effectiveness claims made, and the nature of the organizational context (also see Chapters 2 and 3 for a discussion of these factors). Because a large body of knowledge exists concerning case studies and group comparison designs, only the major considerations for their use in internal evaluation will be described here.

Case Study Designs

Case study designs provide information about outcomes that cannot be acquired through traditional comparison group designs using large numbers of participants. For example, they are used to study a single client or small numbers of persons with rare problems. In these situations, the internal evaluators may use a variety of outcome measures (a) to describe the case in depth, or (b) to describe or replicate the results of a program intervention. For instance, the discovery of fetal alcoholic syndrome and ways of treating it resulted from a series of careful case descriptions. For the purposes of internal evaluation, in situations where a program is highly structured and well controlled, single-case studies are the preferred strategy (Briar & Blythe, 1985; Horn & Heerboth, 1982).

Comparison group studies attempt to control "rival hypotheses" about program effects by using random assignment to make these alternative hypotheses highly unlikely. Case studies attempt to control rival hypotheses by specifying and controlling a limited number of strong alternative explanations, thereby rendering them implausible

(Yin, 1989). In many settings, the use of designs that withhold the program from a comparison group is blocked by legal, ethical, and political considerations. In these situations, case study approaches are often the only feasible alternative (Hersen & Barlow, 1976).

Case studies often permit administering outcome measures (e.g., rating scales, self-monitoring, direct observation) repeatedly over the course of the program. This allows ongoing monitoring and the analysis of the outcomes of individual program components over time. This ongoing monitoring of impacts also may be applied at a systems level. For example, case studies may be used by policymakers to analyze the effects of dissimilar programs by describing the effects of their component parts (Bickman, 1985).

Example: The impacts of the Employment Support Initiatives projects were described and analyzed during their pilot tests in nine different communities (Love & Hagarty, 1985) by monitoring the outcomes of each individual program monthly during the span of the study and by conducting detailed case studies of each site to determine the feasibility of each model. Later, this strategy was extended to evaluate the implementation of nearly 90 employment projects throughout the province of Ontario.

Case studies may be used in either nonexperimental or experimental situations. *Nonexperimental* means that there are no experimental controls. This makes it difficult to exclude factors other than the program when explaining the reasons for client change. As a result, the information from nonexperimental case studies must be interpreted carefully (Kazdin, 1980). The ability to infer results can be strengthened by carefully monitoring the integrity of the program or treatment intervention.

Experimental single-case studies impose control conditions that rule out threats to validity. Experimental designs also can be improved by monitoring the integrity of the program. To reduce threats to internal validity, single case experimental designs measure client outcomes repeatedly before the program to establish a baseline, and then frequently during the program to detect trends. In this way, if client performance differs greatly from the baseline, the internal evaluator will be able to draw stronger inferences about program effects.

Example: The evaluation of a staff treatment program for adolescents monitored the aggressive behavior of each youth for one month to set the baseline rates of disturbance. Next month the staff introduced a program to control aggressive behaviors, and monitoring showed a marked reduction in problem behaviors. Two months later, staff stopped the program, and the frequency of aggressive behaviors for each youth increased toward the baseline rates. After the program was reintroduced a month later, aggressive behaviors diminished again. The staff and consultants concluded that the program was effective in reducing aggressive behaviors with these youths.

To generalize the program effects, the study is usually replicated two to four times with other clients or in other settings. A characteristic of single-case experimental evaluations is *visual analysis* of data, because this design grew out of the operant conditioning tradition, which rarely uses statistical analysis for single-case studies (Parsonson & Baer, 1978). Yin (1989) provides a comprehensive description of case study methods for use in evaluations, as well as numerous illustrations of the use of case studies in fields ranging from policy planning to journalism. Hayes (1981) and Kazdin (1982) also provide useful information about numerous single-case experimental design strategies.

Group Comparison Designs

Group comparison designs are one of the distinguishing features of evaluative research. When senior managers, program planners, and program managers need to make causal claims about program outcomes that are defensible scientifically and logically, they usually examine large group differences through group comparison designs. The evaluators seek to discover lawful relationships between program interventions and client outcomes that follow a predictable pattern despite individual differences among program participants. They do this by comparing the outcomes for a group that receives the program with the outcomes for a control or comparison group that (a) does not receive any program or (b) receives a placebo or alternative program.

Strong causal claims about the impact or effectiveness of a program or treatment are best achieved through "true" experimental designs. These designs employ random assignment of program participants to groups. An internal evaluator wanting to use group comparison designs has to face the considerable problems endemic with using social experimental methods in practice settings (Riecken & Boruch, 1974). For this reason, quasi-experimental designs are often recommended for use in organizational settings (Campbell & Stanley, 1963; Cook & Campbell, 1976, 1979). Quasi-experimental designs also involve comparisons between program and control groups, except that individuals in these groups are not randomly assigned. In place of random assignment, the evaluators select a comparison group matched to the program group on key factors (e.g., age, socioeconomic status) that might modify the outcomes of the program.

For internal evaluation, only a few experimental and quasi-experimental designs are commonly used. The most popular true experimental design for outcome studies is the pretest-posttest control groups design. The pretest permits eliminating alternative explanations for the outcomes, such as history, maturation, and testing and other threats to internal validity.

Example: The internal evaluation unit of a local school board evaluated the intellectual and social development of two groups of preschool children using an attention control group design. The control group received an abbreviated program. This strategy controlled for positive changes in the experimental group that might result simply from the increased attention they received by participating in the program. The children were randomly placed in one of two playgroups: a program group that received a special program for one hour each day, and a control group that watched an educational television program. Both groups were assessed before and after the programs using a battery of standardized tests.

The two most frequently used outcome evaluation designs (Aaronson & Wilner, 1983) for internal evaluation are (a) the quasi-experimental before and after study (pretest-posttest without any control group design), and (b) the pre-experimental "one-shot" study (posttest-only design without control groups). The pretest-posttest design is similar to the previous one, except that the absence of a control group does not permit the evaluation to rule out most of the threats to validity, and, therefore, does not rule out alternative explanations for the measured outcomes. The notable exception is in programs where the changes following the program are unmistakable.

Example: An evaluation of a program designed to teach specific life skills (e.g., using public transportation) to developmentally disabled persons required the participants to demonstrate the skill after receiving the program. Successful demonstration of these skills (i.e., the "signed causes" of Cook & Campbell, 1979) provided a sound basis for inferring that the program produced the outcome.

The "one-shot" design is a pre-experimental design because the simple follow-up study design does not provide any experimental controls.

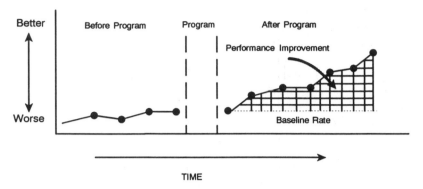

Figure 6.1. Visual Analysis of Time-Series Data

Without a pretest or control group the evaluator cannot be certain that observed outcomes can be attributed to the program. Both of these nonexperimental designs are weak, and they are likely to *overrate* the strength of the outcomes. This follows Hugo Muench's "law" that nothing improves results more than does omitting controls (Bearman, Loewenson, & Gullen, 1974). DerSimonian and Laird (1983) provide a well-known example from a review of the effectiveness of coaching for SAT examinations: Descriptive studies found coaching made a significant difference in performance, matched-control studies noted smaller increases, and randomized-control studies found only slight improvements. Muench's sardonic "law" cautions that a relationship *may* exist between the evaluation *design* and the outcomes of the study. Internal evaluators should be aware of this possibility when designing studies and assessing their findings.

Research findings clearly support the use of simple numerical counts by program managers for monitoring program outcomes. This form of information has been consistently seen by managers, planning team members, and practitioners as credible, useful, and generally easy to collect. Managers usually find time-series designs more credible than pretest-posttest designs because time series measure outcomes at numerous points in time. Time series data lend themselves to visual analysis, which managers find easier to interpret than statistical summaries (see Figure 6.1). Carter (1987) provides several examples of program outcomes that are reviewed periodically by human service organizations:

- number of delinquents who are employed three months
- number of foster children for whom permanency is attained
- number of clients attaining unsubsidized employment

Problems with the use of time-series data include the need to use homogeneous client populations and to make a large number of measurements. The varying baseline and treatment periods across clients also pose a genuine hurdle in some settings.

SELECTING MEASURES AND COLLECTING DATA

Measuring Status Maintenance or Change

For many types of organizations, the concept of client status change is a meaningful way to measure effectiveness: A person purchases a product, makes a sale, acquires a full-time job, returns to prison, or moves from a group home to a supported apartment. Status change measures are widely available, concrete, not easily distorted by rater bias, and, in sum, avoid most of the reliability and validity problems that besiege other outcome measures (Rapp & Poertner, 1987).

Measures of status outcome should be specific, measurable, and understandable. Status outcomes are usually measured by direct observation of a line worker or by client self-reports. In the simplest of terms, there are four major ways of measuring status:

(1) *Binary status.* Was the status outcome present or absent?
(2) *Frequency.* How often did the status outcome occur?
(3) *Duration.* How long did the status outcome last?
(4) *Magnitude or intensity.* How great was the status outcome?

Measuring Goal Attainment

The principal problem has been that goals have been too abstract and measurement methods too complex. A practical method is to define very specific tasks and goals and count them whether achieved or not. The data are then used as a basis for monitoring the progress of individual clients, programs, or entire systems. This method is especially suitable when it is employed in a computer-automated environment (Hudson, 1986).

Using Rapid Assessment Instruments

For ongoing evaluation of client outcomes there must be several additional characteristics beyond the essentials of reliability and validity. They must be short, easy to read, easy to complete, easy to understand, easy to score, and easy to interpret, and they must not suffer response decay on repeated administrations. These may seem to be difficult specifications but considerable progress has been made developing *rapid assessment instruments* (RAIs). RAIs have been designed to measure changes in a wide variety of situations, ranging from intrapsychic factors to family relations (Corcoran & Fischer, 1987; Edelson, 1985; Levitt & Reid, 1981).

Paper-and-pencil *knowledge tests* tailored to the learning goals of a specific program are another form of RAI used to assess educational programs and training interventions. So are *behavioral checklists* that are used by clients, service providers, teachers, significant others (e.g., roommates, relatives), and observers. Often the perspectives of multiple raters are used, particularly in situations where there is pressure for the client to demonstrate a socially desirable behavior (e.g., addiction programs). Behavioral checklists often are used in conjunction with goal setting. In these instances, the client and service provider set goals in behavioral terms and review the attainment of the goal at regular intervals.

RAIs also may be developed by staff to measure such facets of service as continuity of care, level of functioning, and other changes unique to the specific practice setting. Also, specialized RAIs may be developed to reflect client outcomes that are a synthesis of several unique change dimensions.

Example: The staff of a family violence treatment program developed RAIs to measure improvements in batterers' self-esteem, anger control, coping skills, internal locus of control, attitudes toward women, and positive relationships with therapists. The staff created these scales because standardized scales to measure the domains of interest did not exist at that time. Before using the scales for internal evaluation, an external consultant tested the reliability and validity of the scales on a sample of clients.

Measuring Acceptability

Acceptability is a term used to reflect approval by a consumer or a client of a product, service, or program. The term includes the notion of consumer or client satisfaction with services plus other relevant measures, such as clients' ratings of how well the program met their service goals, feedback about the process of service, records of complaints, and commendations. Patti (1985) contends that consumer satisfaction must be a primary outcome for most public and voluntary services. Peters and Waterman (1982) have made the same point for private business. Their advice has not been lost on their audiences, who have made it the cornerstone for marketing the manufacturing and service industries in North America.

The methods required for measuring acceptability are relatively simple and inexpensive. Acceptability studies also are among the most suspect of evaluation methods because they are so frequently abused. They are often poorly designed, using untested questionnaires and biased samples and providing no comparison information (Lebow, 1983a).

Chapter 4 discussed the use of client satisfaction studies for program monitoring. There is general agreement that measures of acceptability used for outcome evaluation must tap several dimensions beyond simple client satisfaction. These dimensions include satisfaction with the plan of service, ratings of goal attainment, skill and attitude of staff, accessibility of services, and follow-up. Lebow (1987) provides a review of simple and well-validated measures of acceptability, such as the Client Satisfaction Questionnaire (Attkisson & Zwick, 1982; Pascoe & Attkisson, 1983), in addition to recommendations for data collection and analysis. Acceptability norms have been developed for several different client populations, and these can be used to judge acceptability with an organization's programs (Lebow, 1983b; Lehman & Zastowny, 1983).

Quality Assurance Reviews

Chapter 4 discussed quality assurance as a method for program monitoring. Although quality assurance initially focused on program structure and staffing (i.e., "inputs"), more recently it has been used for evaluating program outcomes and the process of service delivery. The essence of quality assurance reviews is an ongoing system that (a) identifies patterns of problems with the outcomes of service delivery and then (b) corrects the problems. Quality assurance reviews differ from other quality control processes, such as case supervision or case reviews, in their focus on patterns of problems that transcend the purview of a single worker or program component. Another distinguishing feature is that quality assurance reviews are a *management* responsibility. Typically a senior manager is directly responsible for the quality review process, and senior management is responsible for correcting problems, not just identifying them. A recent trend is to make quality assurance reviews an organizational responsibility by reporting quality review information and corrective action regularly to the organization's board of directors or governing body.

When the effectiveness of a service method or process is the focus of the evaluation, process events can be recorded—such as the length of wait between intake and the initial visit, or whether or not a client file was reviewed within a specified period of time. Methods for quality reviews, therefore, could include case file audits and case reviews directed towards assessing staff compliance with quality standards (Sinclair & Frankel, 1984).

> *Example:* Paul Sherman (1987) offers some simple alternatives to traditional quality assurance methods. Based on an operational definition that quality assurance is the process of judging whether or not staff are making correct decisions about clients, the term *correct* covers the notions of appropriateness, efficiency, and effectiveness. The actual quality assurance indicator is the percentage of clients inappropriately assigned to programs. The data is reviewed semiannually; if performance is inadequate, further analyses may be done to isolate the problem. For example, clinicians who require additional training to improve performance may be identified.

Standardized Measures of Client Outcomes

If simple counts do not reflect whether significant program goals have been achieved, standardized measures may be available. Most standardized instruments are administered by frontline staff who see them as being too complex, requiring too long to administer, or demanding special skill to use. Simple measures of progress and outcome in the evaluation of mental health services are described by Newman, Hunter, and Irving (1987). The value of these simple outcome measures is based on three principles:

Principle 1. Identify the target populations. Scales must be chosen to fit the needs of the major target populations. By selecting a global scale together with a scale suited to each major target group, both service functions (e.g., case management or quality assurance) and administrative functions (e.g., service planning, cost-effectiveness analysis) may be addressed.

Principle 2. Use reliable and valid scales. The empirical literature should be reviewed to identify reliable and valid scales. For example, Jim Ciarlo and his colleagues have compiled a comprehensive review of outcome measures for mental health service delivery and management (Ciarlo, Brown, Edwards, Kiresuk, & Newman, 1986).

Principle 3. Integrate administration and scoring. If correctly integrated into clinical assessment, treatment planning, and case review, the administration and scoring of outcome measures can be managed easily.

Newman, Hunter, and Irving (1987) identify three potential abuses of standardized outcome measures: selecting the wrong scale, careless or purposefully inaccurate use of scales, and the use of outcome data to punish staff. They recommend two essential strategies to prevent these abuses: (a) The scales must be useful for case assessment, planning, and review, and they must be used as part of that process; and (b) senior managers provide a rationale for using the scales and use the scales in program planning and budgeting.

Measuring Environmental Changes

For some programs, the effectiveness of the program must be measured in terms of environmental change. For example, for a developmentally disabled person moving from an institution to a community residence the major outcome is an improved quality of life. Although measurement of environmental impacts is the least developed client outcome area (Rapp & Poertner, 1987), some scales do exist. The Oregon Quality of Life Scale (Bigelow, Brodesky, Steward, & Olson, 1982) and scales of fit between the person and the environment (Kane & Kane, 1984) are examples.

SUMMARY

Effectiveness is a measure of how well a program or organization achieves its intended results. Evaluating program outcomes involves selecting from either case study designs or group comparison designs. The actual design, however, depends on the type of questions asked, the type of effectiveness claims made, and the nature of the organizational context. There are a variety of ways of measuring effectiveness, including *status maintenance, rapid assessment instruments, standardized measures,* and *environmental changes.*

EXERCISES

Use your discussions with the manager and staff to answer the following questions:

1. How does the manager view effectiveness? From your knowledge of the organization, how do you think he or she *should* view effectiveness?
2. What is the attitude of the manager and staff toward evaluating client or consumer outcomes?
3. What types of questions about effectiveness does the program ask? Are these management, evaluative, policy, or research types of questions?
4. Describe the methods the program uses to measure the outcomes of its products or services for its clients or consumers. What types of claims do these methods address?
5. What designs has the program used to evaluate its client outcomes? Were these designs well chosen? What would you propose as two alternative designs?
6. List the measures the program has used to evaluate client or consumer outcomes. What aspects of effectiveness are they measuring? Do the manager and staff agree on the choice of measures? What would they like to change?

7

Evaluating Efficiency

WHAT IS EFFICIENCY?

Effectiveness evaluation concentrates on measuring results, and efficiency evaluation on the use of resources and the process used to obtain those results. *Effectiveness* is doing the right things, and *efficiency* is doing things right (Drucker, 1954, 1974). Even though the net profit declared by a business gives a single measure of both effectiveness and efficiency, it still does not measure all aspects of efficiency. Moreover, in public and nonprofit organizations a single measure of efficiency, such as net profit, does not exist, and performance must be gauged by separate measures for effectiveness and efficiency. Effectiveness and efficiency, therefore, are two measures of output, and they are both crucial measures of performance.

Defining Efficiency

Inputs. In many different types of organizations, profit and nonprofit alike, efficiency is an input-output equation. The primary input is the group of people who create or manage the other inputs, and the primary output is *value to people,* the consumers of services or goods. Input measures are relatively easy to devise and they are useful in measuring effort in terms of the number of staff, meetings scheduled, brochures printed, and other measures of activity.

Outputs. In a business enterprise, outcomes are measured by volume produced or sold and dollars earned. The relationship between input and output is measured by profits—what is left over after all costs are paid. Nonprofit organizations, in contrast, do not have these convenient indicators of outcome and productivity. Measuring outcome and productivity is equally important for nonprofit organizations. For them, however, developing acceptable measures means a considerable investment of time and a keen understanding of the mission of their organization.

Process, product, and results measures. Three key terms are used to classify output measures: (a) process measures, (b) product measures, and (c) results measures. A *process measure* gauges the activities undertaken by the program. The number of planning sessions conducted, the number of training opportunities provided, and the number of public forums organized are examples of process measures. Process measures relate to the organization's efforts. A *product measure* indicates what the organization or program actually does. Other terms are *capacity utilization* and *staff productivity* (Elkin, 1985). When the ratios of outputs to inputs are measured in dollars the term used is *unit costs*. Using the example of a community planning body, improved coordination of services is the organization's mission, a major efficiency goal is to support community planning as economically as possible, and the number of planning sessions conducted is a process measure, whereas the number of plans produced per year is a product measure.

There is a presumption that a causal relationship exists between the organization's activities and the ultimate mission of the organization. A *results measure,* in turn, is a benchmark of output related to the organization's goals. A results measure, however, is not the same as an effectiveness measure (Chapter 6). *Cost outcome* is a results measure that evaluates the costs of accomplishing outcomes over a period of time.

Managers use results measures to improve everyday operations and make them as efficient as possible. If the goal cannot be stated in measurable terms, surrogates or proxies that can be measured quantitatively may be substituted. To continue with the community planning example, the following surrogates may be used to measure the goal of supporting community planning as economically as possible: (a) the number of hours of service provided by volunteer staff; (b) the percentage of travel expenses paid by the participant agencies themselves; and (c) the percentage of operating costs covered by registration fees to special events sponsored by the planning body.

MANAGERIAL ACCOUNTING

For business enterprises, the relationship between input and output is relatively simple. After illustrating the concepts for businesses, here the issues will be addressed for public and nonprofit organizations. The relationship between input and output provides a conceptual framework for the use of evaluation methods related to *managerial economics*

(Horngren, 1987). It can lead to new definitions of program and organizational productivity and performance. The definition of performance is the same for accounting economics and managerial economics, but the perspective of each of these disciplines is different (Anthony & Reece, 1988). Accounting economics measures past performance based on an analysis of the historical record. Managerial economics, in contrast, measures the future consequences of decisions based on current economic data. The objective of managerial accounting is to assist the manager in making good decisions that are congruent with the firm's mission statement. These decisions usually are *alternative choice decisions* that have a financial dimension, such as decisions to expand or reduce a program or to hire regular or temporary staff.

The Marginal Income Model

Alternative choice decisions require managers to answer the question: How will this alternative affect costs and revenues? Because the presence of allocated or indirect costs makes full-cost accounting misleading (Horngren & Foster, 1987), internal evaluators ordinarily use *marginal accounting* for alternative choice decisions.

Example: The full cost of providing services in a certain hospital outpatient clinic is $4,000 per patient per year. This amount includes the clinic's overhead expenses plus a share of the hospital's overhead costs. A decision to reduce the number of patients by 5% will not decrease costs by the same amount, because it is unlikely that salaries and overheads will be lowered much by a 5% reduction in patients.

Marginal accounting recognizes that many costs vary, in whole or in part, with the volume of output. A marginal cost is the amount by which total costs are changed if the volume of output is increased or decreased by one unit. For the outpatient clinic example, it is the cost of including or excluding one patient. The marginal cost includes salaries, materials, energy, expenses, and variable overheads, such as supervisory and maintenance costs that vary with output.

Example: A municipality delivered transportation services for disabled persons, but recently a private firm began providing the services at a lower cost to users. What should the municipality do? The municipality felt that it had an obligation, as articulated in its mission statement, to provide essential services at an affordable rate to special needs populations. In the future the private firm might decide to increase rates or cease services altogether. The marginal income model permitted exploring several alternatives: (a) Continue providing the services at the current fees; projections indicated a loss of one quarter of the users. (b) Reduce the price to keep the current number of users; projections showed a break-even performance. (c) Improve service by coordinating transportation for the disabled with other municipal services (e.g., recreation programs, day treatment programs); marketing studies projected enough users to offset increases in fixed and variable costs and to produce a monthly operating revenue of $20,000. After discussing these and other options, such as contracting out the services, they decided on the third alternative.

This example underscores several key principles in using the marginal income model for the evaluation of efficiency (Magee, 1986). First, decisions must be tied to the mission of the organization. Second, the process evaluates the economic impact of each alternative. Even when precise quantification is not possible, global estimates of trends are useful. Third, improvements usually include increases in output in key areas and changes in operations (e.g., coordination of transportation with other services). Only rarely are improvements limited to cost reductions alone. Finally, techniques based on the marginal income model stress a process that includes participation, dialogue, and feedback. As a result, improvements are more than financial, they are also motivational.

EVALUATING EFFICIENCY GOALS

Organizations are usually planned, operated, and controlled through a hierarchy of interlocking goals (Chapter 5). During the planning process, senior managers decide on the long-term or major goals of the organization and the strategies for reaching them. Although the distinction between overall planning and program planning is usually blurred, the programming process either creates new programs or modifies existing programs to achieve the goals.

An understanding of the hierarchy of interlocking goals is crucial for internal evaluators. A close study of interlocking goals shows that there are two kinds of output measures: process measures and results measures. Process measures of output indicate achievement of program efficiency goals and objectives in terms of the quantity of work accomplished by a program or by a program activity, such as the number of dollars raised, the number of recreation classes given, or the number of hot meals provided.

Results measures focus on the organization's performance in achieving its major goals. Given that output should be related to an organization's goals, some of the more important goals should be stated in quantitative terms, if this is possible. A results measure may be the number of welfare recipients who attain economic independence or the cost of a health care system that may be compared with other measures. Although both types of goals are important in measuring efficiency, achievement of process goals is particularly useful to frontline supervisors and middle managers, and achievement of results goals is important to senior managers.

INTERNAL AUDITING

The aim of management controls is to ensure that the strategic goals of the organization are achieved efficiently and effectively. The operating budget is the chief financial directive for the organization's operations. The approved budget defines a ceiling amount that should not be exceeded, or which lawfully cannot be exceeded. Measuring compliance with the budget is a fundamental evaluation tool. The main foci of the control process should be the program and the responsibility center that implements the program. The emphasis on program control rather than control of the specific resources used (i.e., line-item control), for example, personnel or travel expenses, is an important step forward. The accounting system is the fundamental system for reporting internal operating information.

In larger organizations, internal audits serve as a control for the overall management control system. Compliance auditing is a management tool to help managers operate their programs. The purpose of compliance auditing is to give reasonable assurance to managers that existing financial control procedures are working well. This means reducing the possibility of loss by theft or fraud, ensuring that essential financial information is accurate, and maintaining accountability. The modern process of management controls is largely a self-evaluating system that identifies errors. In turn, compliance auditing provides an independent assessment of the functioning of those controls. Auditors assist managers by evaluating control systems and reporting how well they work.

Some organizations still do not have basic financial and management controls. The results of this situation are displayed daily in reports such as those exposing government waste, improper tendering processes, fictional employees on the payroll, and abuses of the public assistance system. Other organizations have the basic controls, but they expend their energies on strict compliance with accounting rules and neglect procedures for verifying the dependability of information. Problems of accuracy arise when costs are charged to the wrong accounts, whether deliberately or because managers break rules to accomplish the job. Even though it may not be required by law, organizations are becoming aware that external audits are essential to verify the findings of their internal audits.

Does Internal Auditing Have a Role in Evaluation?

The traditional distinction between program evaluation and internal auditing has limited the use of valuable auditing techniques for internal evaluation. In this view, internal auditing focuses on whether the manager has adequate control over a given program. Program evaluation, in comparison, assesses the effectiveness of a program to decide whether it adequately meets current needs and remains a good choice among existing alternatives. Internal evaluation, however, is a management support process that bridges the traditional distinctions between internal auditing and program evaluation (see Schwandt & Halpern, 1988). The methods of internal evaluation are on a continuum spanning these two extremes.

Internal auditing can be a valuable method of internal evaluation and an effective management tool. Contrary to popular belief, the auditing process is not an immutable set of procedures, but a flexible way of telling a story (or building a model) about what has happened and why it has happened. Exclusive emphasis on telling the story of what has happened ("custodial accounting") tends to limit the scope of internal auditing to concerns about accountability for the financial affairs of the organization. This aspect of auditing meets the information needs of many parties, such as boards, stockholders, regulatory bodies, and taxation departments. Although this is an important aspect of internal auditing, forgetting to ask "Why audit?" narrows the range of auditing activities and masks their similarities to other methods of evaluation. Operational and management audits are two tools for increasing the usefulness of audits for problem solving and decision making (Anthony, Dearden, & Bedford, 1988; Comptroller General of Canada, 1989; Comptroller General of the United States, 1981; Cutt, 1988).

OPERATIONAL AND MANAGEMENT AUDITING

Operational auditing partially answers the question of "Why audit?" by investigating whether a program is managing its resources economically and efficiently and by probing the causes of any problems. When conducted properly, operational auditing can show managers how policies and procedures can be improved. Because the analysis of causes requires special expertise, good operational audits are conducted by a multidisciplinary team of persons expert in managing the same type of organization as the one being audited. In some organizations, however, operational audits are still conducted by accountants alone, leading to a discrediting of the audit and its recommendations.

When considered in a broader perspective, operational auditing can be extended further to involve the appraisal of all management activities (e.g., policies, organizational structure, adequacy of planning and control mechanisms) for determining why problems have happened and how they should be corrected. This process is called *management auditing,* although the terms *comprehensive auditing* and *operations analysis* are used as well. Management auditing is a robust process for measuring program efficiency. The purpose of management auditing is to improve program performance and reduce costs by a thorough analysis of all aspects of program management (see Fertakis, 1989). Traditional program evaluation methods rarely, if ever, analyze thoroughly a program's management systems with the intention of identifying worthless or inefficient practices. Management auditing methods are particularly useful for evaluating ongoing service or support activities, such as municipal services or the routine practices of a diagnostic clinic.

Example: The recent savings and loan scandals and the financial crisis in New York City during the 1970s are perhaps the most notorious cases that precipitated operational and management audits. Politicians and taxpayers alike demanded to know what was wrong with the management and control of these systems. They wanted information explaining not only what had happened but also showing what fundamental changes were needed to avoid similar disasters in the future. Operational and management audits were the methods of choice because they are proactive techniques for improving decision making and controls at all levels in the organization.

Process of Management Auditing

Management auditing often is mandated by a governing board or by senior managers as part of a periodic program review cycle. The planned use of management auditing serves to reduce fat that accumulates in any program over time and to set new budget and performance targets for the program until the next review. This use of management auditing fits well with the ongoing nature of internal evaluation activities (Garrison, 1988). The more widely publicized use of management auditing is for "fire fighting" and "damage control" in crisis situations. For example, the "taxpayer's revolt" in the United States in the late 1970s was triggered by widespread allegations of fraud and gross negligence and led to management audits in many municipalities.

Example: The Federal Bureau of Investigation was having difficulty with tracking and monitoring budgetary expenditures in its field offices. An executive assistant director requested a management study of the problem. Operating with a 60-day deadline, the internal evaluation staff worked with four other divisions to develop a management control system and computer software that solved the problem (Sonnichsen, 1988, p. 144).

Getting Managers to Accept Findings

One of the major problems of any management audit is getting managers to accept the findings of the study. This is a familiar variation of the utilization problem endemic to all forms of evaluation. If the program manager has been involved in collaborating in the design of the audit, and has been kept abreast of results, there is a good chance that the manager will accept and adopt the recommendations.

Some management auditors use the ploy of making the recommendations and then delaying the release of the final report for some time (usually six months). The program manager is given time to implement the recommendations. A "progress report" is appended to the final report giving the manager credit for the changes. In this way, the threat to the manager is reduced, and the auditors can promote change while the iron is still hot. Needless to say, selling recommendations, seeing them implemented, and following up are controversial and crucial parts of any internal evaluation (see Barkdoll & Sporn, 1988, for a compelling discussion of strategies for "selling" evaluation results). These broader approaches enable internal auditing to voice eloquently probable future pitfalls and help the manager select safer directions. Internal auditing can speak, therefore, not only the language of accountants, but also that of managers and other professionals from many disciplines who have performance as a top priority. It provides a useful tool to promote effective decision making at all levels in the organization. This is not to say that management auditing and comprehensive auditing are the same as internal evaluation. Rather, internal evaluation may make use of management auditing and comprehensive auditing methods as part of an overall evaluation strategy.

QUANTITATIVE MODELING

An organization is a complex entity comprised of many intertwining systems, functions, and activities. One of the responsibilities of internal evaluation is to provide information to managers about the status of the organization. This is not easy because so many factors interact. Abstractions permit us to simplify reality and see the situation more clearly. Abstractions are also known as *models*. Besides making reality easier to understand, they facilitate planning and decision making by permitting flexible experimentation with alternate scenarios (Nersesian, 1990). The concept of using mathematical models in organizations is not new. Financial reports, for example, are an abstraction or model of the results of the operations recorded by the accounting system. Models are used by evaluators for detecting critical program changes and preparing the organization or program to take advantage of opportunities and avoid serious problems.

Break-Even Analysis

By relating revenues and expenses, a break-even analysis shows at what amount of service delivery or production the total revenue of an organization will match its total expenses. Break-even analysis is an extension of marginal accounting, which was discussed earlier in this chapter. It provides a relatively simple way of modeling revenues and expenses and the variable cost per unit for various levels of output.

Although break-even analysis is often used by businesses to determine the price that gives the desired profit, the technique is useful also for nonprofit organizations. By definition, nonprofits must demonstrate efficient management by balancing their revenues and expenses. Given that variable costs change with volume of service, break-even analysis provides a method of accurately planning services and detecting potential problems.

Linear Programming

In real life situations, managers are faced repeatedly with choosing between programs or activities that compete with each other for limited resources. Linear programming is perhaps the most frequently used method for selecting among alternatives (Gass, 1975). It is based on the premise that the critical variables and limits on their variation can be specified, and that a mathematical model based on linear equations can accurately reflect the relationship among variables. Linear programming is a versatile analytic resource and it may be used for evaluation, administration, marketing, finance, accounting, service delivery, and virtually all decision making situations where the above conditions exist (Levin & Lamone, 1969). In particular, linear programming is a technique for allocating resources or for estimating the optimum combination of resources to achieve a desired goal.

Example: The government of an African nation assigned a part of its budget to rural family planning. The Ministry of Health established a rural family-planning office under the Division of Family Health and Nutrition. By the end of 1988, programs were being delivered through 23 district offices. The quality of transportation and the distances traveled by workers varied greatly from district to district. The ministry questioned the amount of money spent on rural health workers calling on individual families. The internal evaluation unit conducted a series of studies that produced mathematical equations of (a) the relation between the number of families visited and the number of live births, and (b) the relation between the costs of the visits and the costs of transportation and program administration in each district. An analysis was used to develop tables for choosing the number of visits in each district that would minimize the number of births. The evaluation showed that by increasing visits in some districts and reducing them in others an additional 30% decrease in births could be obtained at the same costs. If each district had a skilled internal evaluator, the same methods could be used to select the routes taken by the health workers to minimize the costs of visits.

Simulation

Simulation (also known as "Monte-Carlo") is a very general problem-solving approach that permits the construction of mathematical models that more accurately represent real-world circumstances. Instead of hiring staff, renting space, and evaluating a real program, a computer simulation can simulate the program in less time and with less expense. The actual process of simulation involves using computers to experiment with mathematical models involving elements of probability, such as random client demand or random service times. The essence of simulations is using a random sampling device that simulates chance processes with numerous events (Moskowitz & Wright, 1979; Nersesian, 1989; Thompson, 1976). Because simulations use sampling methods, the results are expressed as statistical estimates, not optimal solutions.

Example: A common use of simulation is for waiting line problems (e.g., customers are waiting to be served, patients to receive treatment, or machines of varying capacity to manufacture goods). A simple example is the waiting period for receiving counseling in a university drop-in counseling center. Students wanting help may or may not wait, and the manager is faced with an unknown flow of clients. Because funding for the counseling center depends on the number of students counseled, the manager does not want to lose those students who will not wait. Using probabilities and random numbers, simulation helps the manager to know the expected cost of various waiting times and to calculate the optimum staffing and service levels.

The value of simulation depends on how well the problem under study can be represented by a mathematical model. Simulation enables the internal evaluator to explore practical decision situations that are beyond the reach of analytic methods. Because simulation inserts uncertainty into the model, it is particularly suitable for models containing risks, unknowns, unpredictable demand, shaky supply, and nonlinear relationships.

Network Analysis

A common problem for managers is making the best possible use of resources to achieve the organization's goals while coping with time and cost limitations. Another common difficulty, however, is the responsibility to manage multiple programs, each with their own set of cost and time constraints. Complex programs can be planned, coordinated, and controlled more efficiently through network analysis techniques. The Critical Path Method (CPM) and the Program Evaluation and Review Techniques (PERT) were responses to this need (Weist & Levy, 1977). Both methods use network analysis, and the acronym PERT is used to embrace both of them. These methods have been used to manage a wide variety of programs and projects, ranging from implementing a new program to controlling auditing programs to marketing new products. Network analysis has the obvious benefit of giving managers the tools to plan the best use of resources to achieve a program goal while considering the constraints of costs and time. Network analysis can identify relationships between tasks and potential problems that are not recognized by other methods. However, network analysis is less effective for new programs that are being designed as they are being implemented.

COMPARATIVE PERFORMANCE OF ORGANIZATIONS

Public and voluntary sector organizations often must justify their efficiency through comparisons with similar organizations. Three major methods are used in these comparisons: (a) performance indicators, (b) cost function models, and (c) models of comparative efficiency, such as data envelopment analysis (Grizzle, 1984).

Performance measurement. Performance measurement is a self-evaluation technique. The organization measures the attainment of its goals using a performance index or ratio composed of a weighted sum of the key goals. Performance measurement has the advantages of being easy to use and interpret and of being usable with a single organization or a small sample of organizations. Because it provides little information about the relationship between inputs and outputs, performance measurement works best when supplemented by an analysis of organizational process, such as a management audit.

Cost function models. Cost function models provide a statistical comparison of the association between inputs and outputs. These models work well if there is a large sample of organizations using the same methods to produce the same goods or services, for example, a hospital or school system. When these conditions exist, performance standards and guidelines for the efficient use of resources can be developed. The major drawbacks of cost function models are the need for large samples of similar organizations and the technical proficiency required to select functions and interpret results.

Example: Internal evaluators in over 20 school boards in a Canadian province developed cost function models of literacy programs for new immigrants. The models included the costs of salaries, fringe benefits, and renting space in the community as well as other important factors, such as teacher training and experience and the immigrants' prior education. The cost function model helped program coordinators understand how the interaction among variables affected efficiency and it guided their decisions concerning the staffing and composition of classes.

Data envelopment analysis. Data envelopment analysis (DEA) uses linear programming techniques to make productivity comparisons among sets of organizations (Charnes, Cooper, & Rhodes, 1981). An organization is considered efficient if the ratio of its weighted outputs to its weighted inputs exceeds or equals the ratios of outputs to inputs of every other organization in the sample. The set of organizations in the sample is used to develop an efficiency frontier composed of all possible linear combinations of efficient organizations and their relative use of resources. The efficiency frontier envelops or surrounds the data points corresponding to the organizations, and DEA derives its name from this characteristic.

DEA has been used successfully in a wide variety of settings, such as hospitals and health care (Sherman, 1984, 1986), education (Bessent, Bessent, Kennington, & Reagan, 1982), and criminal justice (Lewin, Morey, & Cook, 1982). In addition to providing a standardized efficiency score, the DEA technique provides information to managers indicating how efficiency may be improved. DEA enables the use of multiple inputs and outputs while avoiding problems of interdependency (multicollinearity) and specific functional forms. DEA is a promising technique for identifying the comparative efficiency of organizations if a large sample size and technical supports are available.

SUMMARY

Efficiency is the measure of how well an organization converts its inputs (resources) into outputs (programs, goods, services). Internal evaluation uses a wide range of methods to measure efficiency. *Managerial accounting* assists managers in making good decisions that are congruent with the organization's mission statement. Evaluating efficiency goals by measuring the quantity of program activities achieved is a popular approach. *Internal auditing* involves the appraisal of all management activities in determining why problems have happened and how they should be corrected. Good *operational audits* also show managers how policies and procedures can be improved.

Besides auditing approaches, efficiency evaluations make use of quantitative methods, such as *quantitative modeling, break-even analysis, linear programming, simulation,* and *network analysis.* To these may be added methods for comparing the efficiency of similar organizations, including *performance indicators, cost function models,* and *data envelopment analysis.*

EXERCISES

Answer the following questions by using examples from your program:

1. Briefly define the following and give examples: (a) inputs; (b) outputs; (c) process measures; (d) product measures; and (e) results measures.
2. Illustrate with a case example how the program could use the marginal income model to improve efficiency.
3. Write a report addressing each of the following:
   (a) Describe how the program measures efficiency.
   (b) What efficiency goals does the program have?
   (c) What indicators does the program use to measure efficiency goals?
4. If the program has participated in an operational or management audit, describe the scope of the audit and the methods used. Did the manager and staff find the audit process and the audit recommendations useful? What steps in an audit process would you recommend for this program?
5. What types of internal evaluation procedures does the program use to improve the process of delivering its service or manufacturing its product? Select one method of quantitative modeling and describe how it could be used to improve program efficiency in your program.

8

Strategic Benefit

STRATEGIC DECISION MAKING

The last stage of internal evaluation capability is evaluating the ability of a program (or organization) to produce the desired results (i.e., impacts) over an extended period of time. Evaluating long-term impacts is called *social impact evaluation* or *strategic benefits evaluation*. Evaluating strategic benefits is part of the strategic decision making process of senior managers.

The process of strategic decision making involves three key actions: (a) sensing the need for a decision, (b) choosing among alternatives, and (c) implementing the decision. With few exceptions, historically most of the attention has been given to the second stage, variously called strategy formation or strategy formulation. Also, the three steps have been seen as following a serial model in which one step must be completed before the next begins: "Decide first, implement later."

Ansoff (1987) observes that experience has shown several major deficiencies in the serial process model right from the beginning:

1. Both sensing and implementation activities have a determining influence on strategic action. "Marketing myopia" and the inability to gather intelligence information from the environment may delay deciding between alternatives to the point of crisis.

2. Operations management, which is concerned with implementation, and strategic management are strongly interdependent. They exist within the same organization and compete with one another for attention, skills, resources, and money. March and Simon (1958) proposed "Gresham's Law of Planning" to explain this situation: If left uncontrolled, the operational activity suppresses the strategic activity. The close link between implementation and strategic management must be recognized.

3. The serial model is an abstract model that is only one type of observable strategic behavior. For example, Ansoff (1984) notes that the strategic process appears to work more effectively in Japanese organizations, where the components of sensing, deciding, and implementing run in parallel throughout the process.

4. The external environment exerts a major strategic influence because it legitimizes the program or organization. The legitimizing influence is felt in several ways: (a) expectations concerning an organization's contribution to the environment (mission), (b) limits on its strategic degrees of freedom, (c) financial subsidies, and (d) rules of the game that bracket organizational development.

EVALUATING BENEFITS AND COSTS

The distinction between outcomes and benefits is particularly important because each can lead to different conclusions about the effectiveness of programs and strategic decisions.

Example: In a study of tobacco firms, Miles and Cameron (1982) found that the firms had successfully adapted to what is considered to be the most adverse environment ever faced by a U.S. industry. Returns on investment for the "big six" tobacco firms ranged from 9.0% to 17.8% between 1970 and 1979.

In terms of *outcomes*, the firms were highly successful. In contrast, the general public did not favorably evaluate the *benefits* of cigarette manufacturing and the financial success of the tobacco industry. At the time, national polls showed that over 80% of smokers wanted to stop smoking because of the hazards to their health. Also, less than 25% of the public felt that the tobacco industry was concerned about the health and safety of consumers. The subsequent legislation and restrictive public policy governing the tobacco industry may be attributed to an assessment of benefits rather than outcomes. Within the broader social context, benefits are more important than outcomes.

Why Evaluating Benefits Is Crucial

An assessment of the benefits of a program is an essential component of evaluation used in support of the strategic management process. Senior managers are becoming aware that the ultimate survival and growth of a program depends on the benefits it provides and on sensing environmental changes. Benefits are broadly defined in term of overall social impacts. Whereas effectiveness refers to the immediate outcomes of a program, benefit specifies the long-range effects.

Example: The outcomes of an education program include the skills imparted, the number of students graduated, and the certificates awarded. The benefits, however, are the education program's contributions to the success, financial independence, and self-reliance of its students, the community, and the nation.

Managers make day-to-day decisions about the resources and operations of their programs primarily based on program inputs and outputs. Data about program outcomes usually take longer periods of time to collect and analyze, and thus they are more useful for management control decisions. Measuring benefits is essential for strategic decisions, but it requires longitudinal outcome data, and this type of information can be difficult and costly to obtain. To continue the education-program example, longitudinal follow-up data from program graduates may be difficult to collect, given the mobility of young people, the low rate of response to mail surveys, the cost of collecting data from a scientifically credible sample, and the need to safeguard privacy.

Equity

An important yardstick of benefit, particularly in the public and voluntary sectors, is the equity or fairness of the distribution of services. More recently, the business sector is being forced to demonstrate equity of access or face penalties, as evidenced by the heated debates among trading partners such as the United States, Canada, Japan, and Korea. Equity of opportunity within an organization also has become a major management concern, especially with the passing of new hiring and pay equity legislation.

The concept of equity is complex, however, and the internal evaluator must be clear about which aspects are being measured. Savas (1978) described a minimum of five different definitions of equity: equal satisfaction of need, equal payment, equal input, equal output, and equal process.

Equal satisfaction of need. Services are distributed based on need. For example, child welfare workers are sent to communities having high rates of reported child abuse or high risk populations. Snow removal crews are posted to areas with greater than average snowfall. Police are assigned to districts with high crime rates or complaints about police protection.

Equal payment. Consumers pay equally for equal services. As an expectation by the public or as a practical necessity, however, some services are provided free to all persons or on a sliding scale based on need. For example, although private toll roads once existed within cities, now the use of streets and sidewalks is a free public service for all. Senior citizens, students, and the disadvantaged, among others, receive special discounts, tax credits, or grants based on their perceived ability to pay.

Equal input. Inputs or resources are distributed equally. This definition of equity presents several problems. The major difficulty is that people have unequal needs and that unequal inputs may be required to produce the same results for different people. Subsidized day care, school breakfast and lunch programs, and personalized teaching methods recognize this situation and compensate for the economic and social circumstances faced by disadvantaged families. From the perspective of a more affluent family, this solution may not be equitable at all. The harried two-career couple may need affordable quality day care for their child, they may not have time to make a nutritious breakfast or pack a balanced lunch, and their child may benefit from more personal attention or a smaller class size. Even if the equal-input definition is accepted, there is no agreement on the formula for measuring equity. Should it be equal input to each unit area on a per capita basis, or to each neighborhood or district?

Equal output. The criteria for the output level is the same. For example, the availability of hospital beds, the response time for fire alarms, or the frequency of garbage pickups is the same for each area or person.

Equal process. Despite individual differences and the risk of inequitable inputs and outputs, many organizations are expected to provide equity of process. For example, the motor vehicle department expects each person to take the same type of written and driving test before being issued a license. The courts follow due process of law despite the apparent guilt or innocence of a person charged with a crime. This definition fails when systematic bias alters the process, such as when the boss's son is promoted over a better qualified candidate, or when municipal services are provided erratically to a poorer section of town.

Political and Economic Rationality

An organization is a coalition of various stakeholders, each with their set values and intentions, that is held together through a political process. They are part of a coalition that extends outside the boundaries of the organization to include the broader community. Managers and evaluators alike are only beginning to realize they are part of these coalitions. More specifically, the political context, both inside and outside the organization, determines the acceptable levels of effectiveness, efficiency, and equity for that organization or program. Wildavsky (1975) identified political rationality as a crucial criterion of program and organizational performance.

What does political rationality mean? According to Wildavsky, usually the benefits and costs of rival policies and programs are compared strictly in economic terms: Differences in cost and achievement among them are calculated, and one is shown to be more or less efficient than the others. There are other factors that must be considered, including the expense of changing policies and procedures, as well as legal, psychological, or other obstacles that may make the changes impossible. The concept of political rationality considers these costs and their behavioral consequences in an evaluation of strategic benefit (see Campen, 1986; Schmid, 1989). These ramifications include shifts in power relations; an alteration in the "political capital" accumulated over time with politicians, sponsors, funders, and staff; and resistance from persons affected by the changes.

Political rationality implies economic rationality, that is, politically astute actions will ensure adequate resources to operate the organization or program. Economic survival in the face of inflation and recession have given a new importance to the concept of economic rationality. Fiscal responsibility, however, includes more than accumulating funds.

In the private sector, the marketplace permits consumers to choose freely the goods and services they prefer. Economic rationality is not as easy to prove in public and voluntary organizations. Managers of public and voluntary organizations are expected to act as "good stewards" by serving as custodians of public funds. In the absence of open market conditions, managers of public and voluntary organizations have preferred a normative way of allocating resources. These managers seek to demonstrate economic rationality through the use of quantitative methods, such as cost-effectiveness and benefit/cost analyses to assist decision making under conditions of uncertainty. From this point of view, economic rationality and good stewardship are supported by an objective and equitable allocation process. Next we will examine the feasibility of this approach.

SITUATIONAL ANALYSES OF BENEFITS

An analysis of a program's benefits usually begins by examining the external environments that are important to an organization. Areas of study include the macroenvironment, markets, competitors, and other publics. These results are summarized in a *situational analysis* or *environmental scan* that (a) evaluates the implementation of the program in terms of intended and actual benefits, (b) identifies the threats, opportunities, and problems facing the program in the shorter and longer terms, and (c) makes recommendations for changes in strategic direction.

Analysis of the macroenvironment. The term *macroenvironment* conveys the larger political, economic, social, regulatory, and technological environment influencing the organization and its programs. Although these forces cannot be controlled directly, managers must be aware of the forces relevant to their programs. This means they must understand the interaction between the benefits provided by their programs and the fit with the changing macroenvironment.

> *Example:* An employee assistance program has a demonstrated benefit of reducing absenteeism through effective medical and counseling programs. The program's manager must sense the societal trend toward two-career families. In response to this macroenvironmental change, the program may have to offer workplace day care to reduce absenteeism brought about by child care demands.

The key to a successful macroenvironmental analysis is (a) identifying which trends are relevant, (b) limiting the study to areas which will affect the mission and major goals of the program, (c) collecting data about short-term and long-term trends in the broader environment, and (d) controlling for bias when assessing impacts by searching for both opportunities and constraints.

Analysis of strategic markets. Organizations interact with markets or "publics" that are current or potential users of their programs. This is true of private, public, and voluntary organizations. Analysis of benefits requires clearly identifying the markets for the program and analyzing the benefits provided to each market by the program. The major obstacle to undertaking a market benefit analysis is the work involved in questioning each market. The greatest mistake is not assessing each market thoroughly by collecting the following types of information:

- descriptive information about the market, including its size, demographic composition, growth rate, and needs;
- segmentation analysis that identifies the types of persons in each market that come closest to matching the program's goals;
- analysis of the benefits the program offers to each market segment, and a comparative analysis with the benefits offered by competitors;
- analysis of the costs involved in servicing each market;
- analysis of the level of consumer/client satisfaction with the program's services for each market; and
- analysis of the overall reputation, strengths, and weaknesses of the program in comparison with competitors.

Example: Radcliffe and Novak (1986) report on an internal marketing study conducted at Howard Community College to determine employees' evaluation of key educational services provided by the college in 13 areas of service. The study found overall satisfaction with Howard's services but it also identified deficiencies in the registration process, academic advising, and the admissions process.

Analysis of competitors. Nearly every organization or program has competitors, even those in the public and voluntary sector. Even entrenched monopolies such as the postal service receive competition from *generic* competitors, such as courier, telephone, and facsimile services. Voluntary organizations, for example, may find themselves competing for the same donor dollars or volunteer hours. The major competitors should be identified and a careful analysis of their competitive positions should be made by analyzing the benefits they provide to their markets.

Analysis of interorganizational networks. Just as each organization has its competitors, it is likely to have the opportunity and perhaps the necessity to cooperate and forge alliances with other organizations. An organization establishes itself in an interorganizational network by designating staff and money to coordinate work with other organizations. If it provides positive benefits to the broader community, the organization becomes legitimized. With legitimation comes support from managers and staff in other organizations, who convey a positive assessment of the organization to potential clients, professionals, politicians, and funders. Over time, the organization that provides positive benefits carves out its territory or domain. This yields additional advantages: The organization is able to command greater resources than it could justify or produce alone, such as preferential access to specialized funding, community acceptance, and greater professionalization. An analysis of benefits should describe the key interorganizational networks (e.g., associations, professional groups, consumer groups) in terms of the services or resources they provide, and how critical they are to the survival and growth of the organization. Key informant interviews or telephone surveys should be conducted with the network members to identify their perceptions of the benefits provided by the organization, as well as the image and power the organization commands.

BENEFIT/COST ANALYSIS

Benefit/cost analysis is based on the simple idea that a program's benefits should be greater than its costs. Benefit/cost analysis is often used to choose among alternative programs *before* implementation by projecting benefits and costs, and to validate the decision to implement a program *after* it has been in operation long enough to determine its benefits.

Example: A benefit/cost evaluation of a support program for employment disadvantaged persons was used during its first fiscal year of operation to decide whether to proceed with full implementation. The evaluation measured benefits by calculating the amount of social assistance funds the government sponsor would save from the number of persons who had secured permanent employment; it calculated costs by tabulating all expenses related to employment charged to the government. Projections showed that benefits would begin to accrue after one year, and that nearly $3 million would be saved by the second year of operation. The sponsor decided to implement the program in all sites.

In practice, this simple idea has been enshrouded in an complex set of analytic techniques and questionable assumptions. Although benefit/cost analysis has received much criticism, it has been used cogently by private industry and public agencies for decades. There are numerous techniques that are used in benefit/cost analysis, such as capital investment analysis, internal rate of return analysis, and computer modeling. Only the three major techniques appear here. For more information, the reader is referred to the work of Alkin and Solmon (1983), Anthony and Reece (1988), Brealey and Myers (1981), Lyden and Miller (1982), and Thompson (1980).

There are three typical ways of ranking programs in terms of their benefits and costs: (a) benefit/cost ratio; (b) net benefit/cost ratio, or return on investment; and (c) net present value. The benefit/cost ratio is the number representing discounted benefits divided by the discounted costs. The term *discounted* refers to the calculated loss of value of dollars over time, given the assumption that money today is worth less tomorrow. For example, $100 at a discount rate of 10% is worth about $90 one year from now, and just a little more than $80 in two years.

(1) Benefit/Cost Ratio = Discounted Benefits divided by Discounted Costs

Example: A methodone treatment center costs $5,000 per year to treat an addict; if the addict were not treated the costs of crimes, anticrime measures, and lost production would equal $28,000 per year. The benefit/cost ratio is $28,000 divided by $5,000, or 5.6.

(2) Net Benefit/Cost Ratio = Discounted Annual Benefits minus Discounted Annual Operating Costs divided by Discounted Costs

Example: A museum program produces $300,000 in discounted annual benefits less $100,000 in discounted annual operating costs. The discounted capital investment is $175,000. The net benefit/cost ratio is $200,000 divided by $175,000, or 1.14.

(3) Net Present Value = Net Present Value of Benefits minus Net Present Value of Costs

Example: A housing development for the elderly has a present value of benefits of $2,450,000 and a present value of costs of $1,875,000. The net present value is $2,450,000 minus $1,875,000, or $575,000.

The problems with benefit/cost analysis center on a reluctance to accept a single measure of benefit (e.g., dollars) and on difficulties in translating values into monetary terms. Anthony and Young (1988) suggest several key aspects to benefit/cost analysis that do much to reduce the difficulties associated with the technique:

- Because benefit/cost analysis focuses on aspects of a program that can be estimated in monetary terms, it cannot address all aspects of a program's benefits and costs.
- Benefit/cost analysis calls for a systematic analysis of programs and decisions, concentrating upon those decisions that have monetary implications. It is a means of helping responsible persons make decisions, and not a mechanical substitute for good judgment and political wisdom.
- Benefit/cost analysis is likely to be useful under specific circumstances: (a) when goals are clear and there are choices regarding *how* the goal will be met; (b) when the proposal is "economic," such as the choice among several telephone networks; and (c) when programs have equal costs and the question is which one provides the greatest benefits.
- Benefit/cost analysis is not likely to be appropriate: (a) when goals have not been formulated; (b) when goals are unclear; (c) in public and nonprofit programs where managers feel that the benefits cannot be assigned a monetary value; (d) when alternative programs have different missions and goals; and (e) when a causal connection does not exist between the benefits and costs.

PRACTICAL TECHNIQUES FOR
EVALUATING BENEFITS

As part of the strategic decision making process, managers of a wide variety of programs should carefully consider benefits and costs. During program planning and after program implementation, managers must be convinced that the benefits of a program outweigh its costs. Although the comparative benefits and costs may be expressed in general terms rather than as a precise quantitative relationship, this method of approaching programs helps managers focus on the overall value of the program.

Example: Kirkhart and Morgan (1986) in a survey of internal evaluation in 111 community mental health centers found little evidence of evaluations of either benefits or impact on the community. A survey of the internal evaluation units of all 50 state departments of education in the United States conducted by Smith and Smith (1985) also found little use of benefit/cost analysis. This study found the biggest obstacles were difficulties in relating costs to benefits, and an absence of successful examples and training materials to follow.

These examples illustrate that a thorough analysis of long-term benefits and costs may be feasible for only a small percentage of programs, especially in public and voluntary sector organizations. Insistence on the analysis of benefits and costs may stifle trailblazing programs that have not established a causal link between benefits and costs. Likewise, demanding these analyses encourages managers to develop capital-budget or "economic" programs, such as the expansion of a hospital wing or the computer automation of airline reservations. Although these programs may help the organization to run more smoothly, they may have little impact on the program's consumers. The sections that follow describe several simpler methods of obtaining information about the benefits of programs for strategic management purposes.

One of the perpetual tensions in evaluating program benefits is the timing of these studies. Top managers and funders often want the outcomes and benefits assessed shortly after program implementation. Not only are these evaluations premature, but the results may be improperly generalized from a few test sites to the state, province, or nation. Middle and line managers, on the other hand, feel that it takes 3 to 5 years to see the results of a program and 10 years or more to assess its benefits. Even so, they are skeptical that the results of their programs can be separated from other life events and their contributions evaluated with the accuracy required. Furthermore, because the managers consider themselves professionals in their program areas, they want a free hand to control their own programs.

The practical solution to these problems is defining shorter-term outcomes and intermediate indicators of the long-term impacts of the program. Managers first must define a plausible causal chain of events leading to the ultimate benefits of the program, and then define indicators of success at major points along the route. Although these markers of success are not perfect, they focus the evaluation on client needs and the purpose of the program rather than limiting it to resources, services, and the process alone.

Example: One year after graduation students from a university cooperative education program evaluated the relevance of the curricula and the quality of their education in the context of their current and desired work situations. The former students also provided confidential data about their activities that were contributing to the life of the community (e.g., volunteering), as well as about problem behaviors (e.g., drug dependencies, marital conflicts, trouble with the law). Employers also provided a confidential appraisal of the students' performance, and their ratings of how well the university had prepared the students for the workplace. The university used student and employer ratings from students who had not been enrolled in a co-op program to evaluate the comparative benefits and costs of the cooperative education program.

FORECASTING

Forecasting is a special tool for strategic planning. In fact, Henri Fayol, one of the fathers of systematic management, considered forecasting (*prévoyance* or vision) the essence of a manager's work (Fayol, 1929). The value of strategic (long-range) planning in a volatile social and economic climate is hotly contested, and no planning topic is more controversial than forecasting. How, the critics ask, can an organization predict the future with certainty?

The answer is that managers do not need a crystal ball, but a method of evaluating priorities and considering the future in their planning and goal-setting activities. Forecasting uses various techniques to control the amount of uncertainty (Abraham & Ledolter, 1983; Makridakis, Wheelwright, & McGee, 1983). It provides a disciplined way for managers to assess the chances of different events occurring under different conditions, and the probabilities of alternate consequences. Managers, however, cannot be expected to make decisions in a vacuum. Successful forecasting is constructed on a strong foundation of relevant data. This requires the conscientious collection and analysis of data by internal evaluation staff prior to the forecasting efforts of managers. Internal evaluators then use their expertise to facilitate the forecasting process.

Example: As part of the strategic planning process, internal evaluators in a large community service organization forecast the demand for each of its major services or products. Senior managers and the board of directors use this information to modify the organization's strategic direction. They also use it to set objectives about the level of effort and resources required to meet the forecasted demand. The senior managers and board members find that forecasting makes decisions about budget allocation more objective and less vulnerable to lobbying pressures from program managers.

Problems With Forecasting and Some Solutions

If we accept that forecasting is a necessary adjunct to planning, then what is wrong with it? The problem is that much forecasting cannot be trusted. Forecasting is difficult under the best of circumstances, but there seems to be four endemic problems. All of them are linked to the level of evaluation capability (Chapter 3).

Inadequate skills. A shortage of competent internal evaluators in the organization may lead to a lack of valid information to support the forecasting process. The internal evaluators must ask the right questions and obtain data from the right sources. Instead, managers involved in forecasting might have to battle the "turnip factor": Persons involved in collecting the background data did not know what to measure or how to interpret the results.

Inaccurate historical data. An organization must have accurate historical data. This will not be the case if information systems contain data that are poorly defined, collected inconsistently, and reported without any understanding of seasonal cycles and patterns of use.

Incorrect assumptions. Incorrect assumptions about future levels produce inaccurate projections. For example, an internal evaluator may take data from a normal seasonal increase and project it as a trend, thereby making grossly inflated conclusions about the future demand.

Biased data. Internal evaluators may feel tremendous pressure from senior managers to feed data into the forecasting process that support a particular viewpoint or a preordained conclusion.

There are a number of solutions to problems present in forecasting. When the data are collected and analyzed by competent internal evaluators, managers can have confidence that broad trends will be identified, although there may be some disagreement about exact numbers. For additional security, background data for an important forecasting evaluation should include several studies from more than one source, and an independent verification of trends by persons outside of the organization. This doesn't mean a quick telephone call to a few friends: Valid data and objective analysis take time and money. Finally, the results of forecasting should be viewed with healthy skepticism and common sense.

SUMMARY

Strategic benefits evaluation addresses the ability of a program (or organization) to produce the intended results over an extended period of time. Whereas effectiveness refers to the immediate outcomes of a program, *benefit* specifies the long-range effects. In addition to *social impacts,* measures of benefits include *equity* and *political and economic rationality.*

An analysis of benefits usually begins with an environmental scan, consisting of a situational analysis of the organization's external environment. The benefit/cost analysis follows, comprising a systematic analysis of programs and decisions, and concentrating upon those decisions that have monetary implications. Benefit/cost analysis is likely to be most useful when goals are clear, when there are choices regarding how the goal will be met, and when those choices can be cast in monetary terms.

One of the perpetual tensions in evaluating program benefits is the timing of these studies. Top managers and funders often want the outcomes and benefits assessed shortly after program implementation. Middle and line managers, in contrast, feel that it takes 3 to 5 years to see the results of a program and 10 years or more to assess its benefits. The practical solution to these problems is phasing the benefit/cost analysis by defining shorter-term outcomes and intermediate indicators of the long-term impacts of the program.

EXERCISES

1. Describe (a) the process of evaluating strategic position, (b) how outcomes and benefits are different, and (c) why evaluating long-term impacts and strategic benefits is crucial to the survival and growth of the organization. How does your organization evaluate strategic benefits?

2. Imagine you are a senior manager in three different types of organizations: (a) a hospital, (b) a community college, and (c) a fire department. After reviewing the different meanings of equity, describe how the concept may be measured in each of the organizations.

3. What is meant by equity and by political and economic rationality? After interviewing the manager in your organization describe how these factors enter into the manager's evaluation decisions.

4. Together with the manager and staff, conduct a situational analysis and describe the benefits/cost profile of the program. Use diagrams to illustrate. What are the pros and cons of using benefit/cost analysis for evaluating this program?

References

Aaronson, N. K., & Wilner, D. M. (1983). Evaluation and outcome research in community mental health centers. *Evaluation Review, 7,* 303-320.

Abraham, B., & Ledolter, J. (1983). *Statistical methods for forecasting.* New York: John Wiley.

Adams, K. (1985). Gamesmanship for internal evaluators: Knowing when to "hold 'em" and when to "fold 'em". *Evaluation and Program Planning, 8,* 53-57.

Adie, R. F. & Thomas, P. G. (1987). *Canadian public administration: Problematical perspectives.* Toronto, ON: Prentice-Hall.

Alkin, M., & Solmon, L. (Eds.). (1983). *The costs of evaluation.* Beverly Hills, CA: Sage.

Ansoff, H. I. (1984). *Implanting strategic management.* New York: Prentice-Hall.

Ansoff, H. I. (1987). The emerging paradigm of strategic behavior. *Strategic Management Journal, 8,* 501-515.

Anthony, R. (1965). *Planning and control systems: A framework for analysis.* Boston: Graduate School of Business Administration, Harvard University.

Anthony, R., Dearden, J., & Bedford, N. M. (1988). *Management control systems* (6th ed.). Homewood, IL: Irwin.

Anthony, R., & Reece, J. (1988). *Accounting: Text and cases* (8th ed.). Homewood, IL: Irwin.

Anthony, R., & Young, D. (1988). *Management control in nonprofit organizations* (4th ed.). Homewood, IL: Irwin.

Attkisson, C. C., & Broskowski, A. (1978). Evaluation and the emerging human service concept. In C. C. Attkisson, W. A. Hargreaves, M. J. Horowitz, and J. E. Sorensen (Eds.), *Evaluation of human service programs.* New York: Academic Press.

Attkisson, C. C., & Hargreaves, W. A. (1977). A conceptual model for program evaluation in health organizations. In H. C. Schulberg & F. Baker (Eds.), *Program evaluation in the health fields* (Vol. 2). New York: Behavioral Publications.

Attkisson, C. C., Hargreaves, W. A., Horowitz, M. M., & Sorensen, J. E. (Eds.). (1978). *Evaluation of human service programs.* New York: Academic Press.

Attkisson, C. C., & Zwick, R. (1982). The Client Satisfaction Questionnaire. *Evaluation and Program Planning, 5,* 233- 237.

Baggozi, R. P. (1979). Toward a formal theory of marketing exchanges. In O. C. Ferrell, S. W. Brown, and C. W. Lamb, Jr., *Conceptual and theoretical developments in marketing,* (pp.431-447). Chicago: American Marketing Association.

Barkdoll, G., & Sporn, D. (1988). Federal evaluation in an executive environment: Two programmatic principles. In C. Wye & H. Hatry (Eds.), *Timely, low-cost evaluation in the public sector* (pp. 63-72). San Francisco: Jossey-Bass.

Barnard, C. I. (1938). *The functions of the executive.* Cambridge, MA: Harvard University Press.

Bass, R. D. & Windle, C. (1972). Continuity of care: An approach to measurement. *American Journal of Psychiatry, 129,* 196-201.

Bearman, J. E., Loewenson, R. B., & Gullen, W. H. (1974). *Muench's postulates, laws, and corollaries, or Biometricians' views on clinical studies* (Biometrics Note No. 4.).

139

Bethesda, MD: Office of Biometry and Epidemiology, National Eye Institute, National Institutes of Health.

Becker, G. S. (1977). *The economic approach to human behavior.* Chicago: University of Chicago Press.

Bessent, A., Bessent, W., Kennington, J., & Reagan, B. (1982). An application of mathematical programming to assess productivity in the Houston independent school district. *Management Science, 28*(12), 1355-1367.

Bickman, L. (1985). Improving established statewide programs: A component theory of evaluation. *Evaluation Review, 9*(2), 189-208.

Bigelow, D. A., Brodesky, G., Steward, L., & Olson, M. (1982). The concept and measurement of quality of life as a dependent variable in evaluation of mental health services. In G. J. Stohler & W. R. Tash (Eds.), *Innovative approaches to mental health education* (pp. 345-366). New York: Academic Press.

Blanchard, M., & Tager, M. (1985). *Working well.* New York: Simon & Schuster.

Bocialetti, G., & Kaplan, R. E. (1986). "Self-study" for human service agencies: Managing a three-sided relationship. *Evaluation and Program Planning, 9,* 1-11.

Bolin, D., & Kivens, L. (1975). Evaluation in a community mental health center: Hennepin County Mental Health Service. *Evaluation, 2*(2), 60-63.

Brealey, R., & Myers, S. (1981). *Principles of corporate finance.* New York: McGraw-Hill.

Briar, S., & Blythe, B. (1985). Agency support for evaluating the outcomes of social work services. *Administration in Social Work, 9,* 25-36.

Burstein, L. (1984). The use of existing data bases in program evaluation and school improvement. *Educational Evaluation and Policy Analysis, 6,* 307-318.

Calder, B. J. (1977). Focus groups and the nature of qualitative marketing research. *Journal of Marketing Research, 14,* 353-364.

Calsyn, R. J. & Davidson, W. S. (1978). Do we really want a program evaluation strategy based solely on individualized goals? A critique of Goal Attainment Scaling. *Community Mental Health Journal, 14* (4), 300-308.

Campbell, D. T., & Stanley, J. C. (1963). *Experimental and quasi-experimental designs for research.* Chicago: Rand McNally.

Campen, J. T. (1986). *Benefit, cost, and beyond: The political economy of benefit-cost analysis.* Cambridge, MA: Ballinger.

Carter, R. (1983). *The accountable agency.* Beverly Hills, CA: Sage.

Carter, R. (1987). Measuring client outcomes: the experience of the states. *Administration in Social Work, 11* (3/4), 73-88.

Charnes, A., Cooper, W. W., & Rhodes, E. (1981). Evaluating program and managerial efficiency: An application of data envelopment analysis to program follow through. *Management Science, 27* (6), 668-697.

Chelimsky, E. (1985). Program evaluation and the use of extant data. In L. Burstein, H. E. Freeman, & P. H. Rossi (Eds.), *Collecting evaluation data: Problems and solutions.* Beverly Hills, CA: Sage.

Ciarlo, J. A. (1982). Accountability revisited: The arrival of client outcome evaluation. *Evaluation and Program Planning, 5,* 31-36.

Ciarlo, J. A., Brown, T. R., Edwards, D. W., Kiresuk, T. J., & Newman, F. L. (1986). *Assessing mental health treatment outcome measurement techniques* (National Institute of Mental Health, Series FN No. 9, DDHS Pub. No. [ADM] 86-1301). Washington, DC: Superintendent of Documents, U.S. Government Printing Office.

Clifford, D. L. (1987). A consideration of simple measures and organizational structure. *Evaluation and Program Planning, 10,* 231-237.

Clifford, D. L. & Sherman, P. (1983). Internal evaluation: Integrating program evaluation and management. In A. J. Love (Ed.), *Developing effective internal evaluation* (pp. 23-45). San Francisco: Jossey-Bass.

Cochran, N. (1979). On the limiting properties of social indicators. *Evaluation and Program Planning, 2,* 1-4.

Cohen, J. (1977). *Statistical power analysis for the behavioral sciences* (rev. ed.). New York: Academic Press.

Comptroller General of Canada, Program Evaluation Branch (1989). *Working standards for the evaluation of programs in federal departments and agencies.* Ottawa, ON: Supply & Services Canada.

Comptroller General of the United States. (1981). *Standards for audit of government organizations, programs, activities and functions.* Washington, DC: Government Printing Office.

Cook, T. D., & Campbell, D. T. (1976). The design and conduct of quasi-experiments and true experiments in field settings. In M. D. Dunnette (Ed.), *Handbook of industrial and organizational research.* Skokie, IL: Rand McNally.

Cook, T. D., & Campbell, D. T. (1979). *Quasi-experimentation: Design and analysis issues for field settings.* Skokie, IL: Rand McNally.

Corcoran, K., & Fischer, J. (1987). *Measures for clinical practice: A sourcebook.* New York: Free Press.

Crosby, P. B. (1979). *Quality is free: The art of making quality certain.* New York: Mentor.

Crosby, P. B. (1985). *Quality without tears: The art of hassle free management.* New York: Plume.

Cutt, J. (1988). *Comprehensive auditing in Canada: Theory and practice.* New York: Praeger.

Cyert, R. M., & March, J. G. (1963). *A behavioral theory of the firm.* Englewood Cliffs, NJ: Prentice-Hall.

Delbecq, A. L., Van de Ven, A. H., & Gustafson, D. H. (1975). *Group techniques for programme planning: A guide to the nominal group technique and Delphi processes.* Glenview, IL: Scott, Foresman.

DerSimonian, R. & Laird, N. M. (1983). Evaluating the effect of coaching on SAT scores: a meta-analysis. *Harvard Educational Review, 53,* 1-15.

Dillon, J. T. (1984). *Finding the question for evaluation research* (ROEP Rep. No. 102). Portland, OR: Northwest Regional Educational Laboratory.

Driver, M. & Rowe, A. (1979). Decision making styles: A new approach to management decision making. In C. Copper (Ed.), *Behavioral problems in organization* (chap. 6). Englewood Cliffs, NJ: Prentice-Hall.

Drucker, P. F. (1954). *The practice of management.* New York: Harper & Row.

Drucker, P. F. (1974). *Management: Tasks, responsibilities, practices.* New York: Harper & Row.

Dunn, W. N. (1982). Reforms as arguments. *Knowledge: Creation, Diffusion, Utilization, 3* (3), 293-326.

Dunphy, D. C. (1981). *Organizational change by choice.* Sydney: McGraw-Hill.

Edelson, J. L. (1985). Rapid assessment instruments for evaluating practice with children and youth. *Journal of Social Service Research, 8* (3), 17-31.

Elkin, R. (1985). Playing the piper and calling the tune: Accountability in the human services. *Administration in Social Work, 9* (2), 1-13.

Evaluation Research Society Standards Committee. (1982). Evaluation Research Society standards for program evaluation. In P. H. Rossi (Ed.), *Standards for evaluation practice* (pp. 17-19). San Francisco: Jossey-Bass.

Fayol, H. (1929). *General and industrial management.* (J. A. Conbrough, Trans.). Geneva: International Management Institute.

Fertakis, J. P. (1989). *The design and implementation of administrative controls: A guide for financial executives.* New York: Quorum.

Fiester, A. R. (1978). The Access System: A procedure for evaluating children's services at community mental health centers. *Community Mental Health Journal, 14* (3), 224-232.

Flay, B. R., & Best, J. A. (1982). Overcoming design problems in evaluating health behavior programs. *Evaluation and the Health Professions, 5* (1), 43-69.

Friedel, J., & Papik, N. (1986). *The eastern Iowa community college district program evaluation process* (revised). Bettendorf: Eastern Iowa Community College District.

Galbraith, J. (1973). *Designing complex organizations.* Reading, MA: Addison-Wesley.

Galbraith, J. (1977). *Organizational design.* Reading, MA: Addison-Wesley.

Galbraith, J. (1982, Winter). Designing the innovative organization. *Organizational Dynamics,* 5-25.

Garrison, R. H. (1988). *Managerial accounting: Concepts for planning, control, and decision making* (5th ed.). Homewood, IL: Business Publishers.

Gass, S. (1975). *Linear programming* (4th ed.). New York: McGraw-Hill.

Gibb, C. A. (1954). Leadership. In G. Lindsey (Ed.), *Handbook of social psychology* (Vol. 2). Reading, MA: Addison-Wesley.

Glaser, E. M., & Kirkhart, K. E. (1982). *Descriptive analyses of preassessment data* (HIRI Technical Report). Austin, TX: Human Interaction Research Institute.

Graen, G. (1977). Effects of linking pin quality on the quality of working life of lower participants. *Administrative Science Quarterly, 22,* 491-504.

Grandori, A. (1984, June). A prescriptive contingency view of organizational decision making. *Administrative Science Quarterly,* 192-209.

Grant, D. L. (Ed.). (1978). *Monitoring ongoing programs.* San Francisco: Jossey-Bass.

Grizzle, G. A. (1984, March-April). Developing standards for interpreting agency performance: An exploration of three models.*Public Administration Review,* 128-133.

Guba, E. (1969). The failure of educational evaluation. *Educational Technology, 9,* 29-38.

Haimann, T., Scott, W. G., & Connor, P. E. (1978). *Managing the modern organization* (3rd ed.). Boston: Houghton Mifflin.

Hargreaves, W. A. (1982). Outcome evaluation or treatment research? A response to Ciarlo. *Evaluation and Program Planning, 5,* 354-358.

Harrison, M.I.(1987). *Diagnosing organizations.* Beverly Hills, CA: Sage.

Hayes, S. C. (1981). Single case experimental design and empirical clinical practice. *Journal of Consulting and Clinical Psychology, 49,* 193-211.

Hegarty, T. W. & Sporn, D. L. (1988). Effective engagement of decisionmakers in program evaluation. *Evaluation and Program Planning, 11,* 335-339.

Hersen, M., & Barlow, D. (1976). *Single case experimental designs: Strategies for studying behavior change.* New York: Pergamon.

Hill, E., & Hill, M. (1983). The use of the Discrepancy Evaluation Model in evaluating educational programs for visually handicapped persons. *Education of the Visually Handicapped, 15* (1), 2-11.

Hodder, J., & Riggs, H. (1985, January-February). Pitfalls in evaluating risky projects. *Harvard Business Review,* 128-135.

Hopwood, A. (1974). *Accounting and human behavior.* Englewood Cliffs, NJ: Prentice-Hall.

Horn, W. F., & Heerboth, J. (1982). Single case experimental designs in program evaluation. *Evaluation Review, 9* (2), 189-208.

Horngren, C. T. (1987). *Introduction to management accounting* (7th ed.). Englewood Cliffs, NJ: Prentice-Hall.

Horngren, C. T., & Foster, G. (1987). *Cost-accounting: A managerial emphasis.* Englewood Cliffs, NJ: Prentice-Hall.

House, E. R. (1986). Internal evaluation. *Evaluation Practice, 7,* 63-64.

Hudson, W. W. (1986). *Computer assisted management assessment system.* Tallahassee, FL: WALYMR Publishing.

Hudson, W. W. (1987). Measuring clinical outcomes and their use for managers. *Administration in Social Work, 11* (3/4), 59-71.

Huse, E. (1966, Winter). Putting in a management development program that works. *California Management Review, 9,* 73-80.

Huse, E., & Cummings, T. (1985). *Organization development* (3rd ed.). St. Paul, MN: West.

Huse, E., & Kay, E. (1964). Improving employee productivity through work planning. In J. Blood (Ed.), *The personnel job in a changing world* (pp. 301-315). New York: American Management Association.

Joyce, W. F. (1986, September). Matrix organization: A social experiment. *Academy of Management Journal,* 536-561.

Kamis, E. (1981). Sound, targeted compassion: Assessing the needs of and planning services for deinstitutionalized clients. In I. D. Rutman (Ed.), *Planning for deinstitutionalization: A review of principles, methods, and applications* (Human Services Monograph Series, No. 28.). Washington, DC: Project SHARE, Department of Health and Human Services.

Kane, R. A., & Kane, R. L. (1984). *Assessing the elderly.* Lexington, MA: Lexington.

Kaufman, R. (1982). *Identifying and solving problems: A systems approach* (3rd ed.). San Diego, CA: University Associates.

Kaufman, R., & English, F. W. (1979). *Needs assessment: Concept and application.* Englewood Cliffs, NJ: Educational Technology Publications.

Kazdin, A. E. (1980). *Research design in clinical psychology.* New York: Harper & Row.

Kazdin, A. E. (1982). *Single case research designs: Methods for clinical and applied settings.* New York: Oxford.

Kennedy, M. M. (1983). The role of the in-house evaluator. *Evaluation Review, 7* (4), 519-541.

Kimmel, A. J. (1988). *Ethics and values in applied social research.* Newbury Park, CA: Sage.

Kiresuk, T. (1973). Goal attainment scaling at a county mental health service. *Evaluation, 1,* 12-18.

Kiresuk, T., & Lund, S. (1975). Process and outcome measurement using goal attainment scaling. In J. Zusman & C. R. Wurster (Eds.), *Program evaluation: Alcohol, drug abuse, and mental health services.* Lexington, MA: Lexington.

Kiresuk, T., & Sherman, R. (1968). Goal attainment scaling: A general method for evaluating comprehensive community mental health programs. *Community Mental Health Journal, 4,* 443-453.

Kirkhart, K. E. (1979). *Program evaluation in community mental health centers.* Ph.D. dissertation, University of Michigan.

Kirkhart, K. E., & Morgan, R. O. (1986). Evaluation in mental health centers: Assessing the hierarchical model. *Evaluation Review, 10* (1), 127-141.

Kolb, D. A., & Frohman, A. L. (1970). An organization development approach to consulting. *Sloan Management Review, 12,* 51-65.

Korn, S. W. (1982). How evaluators can deal with role conflict. *Evaluation and Program Planning, 5,* 53-58.

Krech, D. (Ed.). (1946). Action and research—a challenge. *Journal of Social Issues, 2* (4), 1-79.

Landsberg, G. (1983). Program utilization and service utilization studies: A key tool for evaluation. In A. J. Love (Ed.), *Developing effective internal evaluation* (pp. 93-100). San Francisco: Jossey-Bass.

Larsen, D., Attkisson, C., Hargreaves, W., & Nguyen, T. (1979). Assessment of client/patient satisfaction: Development of a general scale. *Evaluation and Program Planning, 2,* 197-207.

Latham, G. P., & Locke, E. A. (1979, Autumn). Goal setting—a motivational technique that works. *Organizational Dynamics, 8,* 68-80.

Lavrakas, P. (1987). *Telephone survey methods: Sampling, selection, and supervision.* Newbury Park, CA: Sage.

Lawler, E., & Mohrman, S. (1985, January-February). Quality circles after the fad. *Harvard Business Review,* 65-71.

Lawler, E., Nadler, D., & Cammann, C. (Eds.). (1980). *Organizational assessment.* New York: John Wiley.

Lebow, J. (1983a). Methodological considerations in the assessment of consumer satisfaction with mental health treatment. *Evaluation Review, 7,* 729-752.

Lebow, J. L. (1983b). Research assessing consumer satisfaction with mental health treatment: A review of findings. *Evaluation and Program Planning, 6,* 211-236.

Lebow, J. L. (1987). Acceptability as a simple measure in mental health program evaluation. *Evaluation and Program Planning, 10,* 191-195.

Lehman, A. F., & Zastowny, T. R. (1983). Patient satisfaction with mental health services: A meta-analysis to establish norms. *Evaluation and Program Planning, 6,* 265-274.

Levin, R. I., & Lamone, R. L. (1969). *Linear programming for management decisions.* Homewood, IL: Irwin.

Levitt, J. L., & Reid, W.J. (1981). Rapid assessment instruments for practice. *Social Work Research and Abstracts, 17* (1), 13-19.

Lewin, K. (1948). *Resolving social conflicts.* New York: Harper.

Lewin, A. Y., Morey, R. C., & Cook, T. J. (1982). Evaluating the administrative efficiency of courts. *Omega, 10* (4), 401-426.

Love, A. J. (Ed.). (1983a). *Developing effective internal evaluation.* San Francisco: Jossey-Bass.

Love, A. J. (1983b). The organizational context and the development of internal evaluation. In A. J. Love (Ed.), *Developing effective internal evaluation* (pp. 5-22). San Francisco: Jossey-Bass.

Love, A. J., & Hagarty, S. F. (1985). The employment support initiatives projects: A participatory approach to evaluation. *Canadian Journal of Community Mental Health, 4* (2), 99-114.

Lovelock, C., & Weinberg, C. (1984). *Marketing for public and nonprofit managers.* New York: John Wiley.

Lyden, F., & Miller, E. (Eds.). (1982). *Public budgeting: Program planning and implementation* (4th ed.). Englewood Cliffs, NJ: Prentice-Hall.

Magee, R. P. (1986). *Advanced managerial accounting.* New York: Harper & Row.

Makridakis, S., Wheelwright, S., & McGee, V. (1983). *Forecasting: Methods and applications* (2nd ed.). New York: John Wiley.

March, J. G., & Simon, H.A. (1958). *Organizations.* New York: Wiley.

McCullough, P. (1975). Training for evaluators. In J. Zusman & C. R. Wuster (Eds.), *Program evaluation in alcohol, drug abuse, and mental health* (pp. 247-266). Lexington, MA: D. C. Heath.

McGregor, D. (1957, May-June). An uneasy look at performance appraisal. *Harvard Business Review, 35,* 89-94.

McHugh, R. D., Jr. (1986, August). The auditor as internal consultant. *The Internal Auditor,* 46-48.

McKillip, J. (1987). *Needs analysis: Tools for the human services and education.* Newbury Park, CA: Sage.

Miles, R. H. & Cameron, K. S. (1982). *Coffin nails and corporate strategies.* Englewood Cliffs, NJ: Prentice-Hall.

Mintzberg, H. (1975, July-August). The manager's job: Folklore and fact. *Harvard Business Review.*

Mintzberg, H. (1980). *The nature of managerial work.* Englewood Cliffs, NJ: Prentice-Hall.

Misanchuk, E. R. (1984). Analysis of multi-component educational and training needs. *Journal of Instructional Development, 7,* 28-33.

Mogensen, A. H. (1963). Work simplification: A programme of continuous improvement. In H. B. Maynard (Ed.), *Industrial engineering handbook* (2nd ed., pp. 183-191). New York: McGraw-Hill.

Mohr, W., & Mohr, H. (1983). *Quality circle: Changing images of people at work.* Reading, MA: Addison-Wesley.

Moore, C. (1987). *Group techniques for idea building.* Newbury Park, CA: Sage.

Moskowitz, H., & Wright, G. P. (1979). *Operations research techniques for management.* Englewood Cliffs, NJ: Prentice-Hall.

Nadler, D., Mirvis, P., & Cammann, C. (1976, Spring). The on-going feedback system: Experimenting with a new management tool. *Organizational Dynamics, 4* (4), 63-80.

Neigher, W. D., & Metlay, W. (1983). Values and methods: Evaluation and management perspectives. In A. J. Love (Ed.), *Developing effective internal evaluation* (pp. 47-60). San Francisco: Jossey-Bass.

Nersesian, R. L. (1989). *Computer simulation in business decision making: A guide for managers, planners, and MIS professionals.* New York: Quorum.

Nersesian, R. L. (1990). *Corporate planning, human behavior, and computer simulation: forecasting business cycles.* New York: Quorum.

Newman, F. L., Heverly, M., Rosen, M., Kopta, S. M., & Bedell, R. (1983). Influences on internal evaluation data dependability: Clinicians as a source of variance. In A. J. Love (Ed.), *Developing effective internal evaluation* (pp. 71-92). San Francisco: Jossey-Bass.

Newman, F. L., Hunter, R. H., & Irving, D. (1987). Simple measures of progress and outcome in the evaluation of mental health services. *Evaluation and Program Planning, 10,* 209-218.

Newman, H., O'Reilly, W., & Van Wijk, A. (1987). *Self-evaluation and planning for human service organizations.* New York: American Management Association.

Newman, F. L., White, R., Zuskar, D., & Plaut, E. (1983). Influences on internal evaluation data dependability: Organizational issues and data quality control. In

A. J. Love (Ed.), *Developing effective internal evaluation* (pp. 61-69). San Francisco: Jossey-Bass.

Novak, J. D., & Gowin, D. B. (1984). *Learning how to learn.* New York: Cambridge University Press.

Odiorne, G. S. (1965). *Management By Objectives: A system of management leadership.* New York: Pitman.

Parsonson, B. D. & Baer, D. M. (1978). The analysis and presentation of graphic data. In T. R. Kratochwill (Ed.), *Single subject research: Strategies for evaluating change.* New York: Academic Press.

Pascoe, G. C., & Attkisson, C. C. (1983). The Evaluation Ranking Scale: A new methodology for assessing satisfaction. *Evaluation and Program Planning, 4,* 139-150.

Patti, R. (1983). *Social welfare administration.* Englewood Cliffs, NJ: Prentice-Hall.

Patti, R. (1985). In search of purpose for social work administration. *Administration in Social Work, 9* (3), 1-4.

Patti, R. (1987). Managing service effectiveness in social welfare: A performance model. *Administration in Social Work, 11* (3/4), 7-21.

Patton, M. Q. (1982). *Practical evaluation.* Beverly Hills, CA: Sage.

Peach, H. G., & Hirst, E. (1989). Factors in the practice, organization, and theory of evaluation. *Evaluation and Program Planning, 12,* 163-170.

Peters, T. J., & Waterman, R., Jr. (1982). *In search of excellence.* New York: Harper & Row.

Peters, T. J., & Austin, N. (1986). *A passion for excellence.* London: Fontana.

Porter, E. (1989). Using existing databases: A case study. *The Canadian Journal of Program Evaluation, 4* (1), 27-38.

Radcliffe, S., & Novak, V. (1986). *Howard Community College 1986 staff services evaluation: Internal marketing survey* (Research Report No. 45). Columbia, MD: Howard Community College, Office on Institutional Research.

Radin, B. A. (1987). The organization and its environment: What difference do they make? In J. S. Wholey (Ed.), *Organizational excellence: Stimulating quality and communicating value* (pp. 165-177). Lexington, MA: Lexington.

Rapp, C. A., & Poertner, J. (1987). Moving clients center stage through the use of client outcomes. *Administration in Social Work, 11* (3/4), 23-38.

Riecken, H., & Boruch, R. (Eds.). (1974). *Social experimentation.* New York: Academic Press.

Rossi, P., & Freeman, H. (1982). *Evaluation: A systematic approach* (2nd ed.). Beverly Hills, CA: Sage.

Rothman, J. (1980). *Using research in organizations: A guide to successful application.* Beverly Hills, CA: Sage.

Rowland, A. D. (1984). Combining quality circles and work simplification. *Training and Development Journal, 38* (1), 90- 91.

Rutman, L. (1980). *Planning useful evaluations: Evaluability assessment.* Beverly Hills, CA: Sage.

Savas, E. S. (1978). On equity in providing public services. *Management Science, 24,* 800-808.

Sayles, L. (1964). *Managerial behavior.* New York: McGraw-Hill.

Schein, E. H. (1969). *Process consultation: Its role in organizational development.* Reading, MA: Addison-Wesley.

Schmid, A. A. (1989). *Benefit cost analysis: A political economy approach.* Boulder, CO: Westview.

Schmidt, R. R., Scanlon, J. W., & Bell, J. B. (1979). *Evaluability assessment.* Rockville, MD: Project SHARE, DHEW No. 05-76-730.

Schwandt, T. A., & Halpern, E. S. (1988). *Linking auditing and metaevaluation: Enhancing quality in applied research.* Newbury Park, CA: Sage.

Scriven, M. (1980). *The logic of evaluation.* Pt. Reyes, CA: Edge.

Seashore, S., Lawler, E., Mirvis, P., & Cammann, C. (Eds.). (1983). *Assessing organizational change.* New York: John Wiley.

Sechrest, L., West, S., Phillips, M., Redner, R., & Yeaton, W. (1979). Some neglected problems in evaluation research: strength and integrity of treatments. *Evaluation Studies Review Annual* (Vol. 4). Beverly Hills,CA: Sage.

Sherman, H. D. (1984). Hospital efficiency measurement and evaluation: Empirical test of a new technique. *Medical Care, 22* (10), 922-938.

Sherman, H. D. (1986). Managing productivity of health care organizations. In R. H. Silkman (Ed.), *Measuring efficiency: Data envelopment analysis* (pp. 31-46). San Francisco: Jossey-Bass.

Sherman, P. (1987). Simple quality assurance measures. *Evaluation and Program Planning, 10,* 227-229.

Sieber, J. E. (1980). Being ethical: Professional and personal decisions in program evaluation. In R. Perloff & E. Perloff (Eds.), *Values, ethics, and standards in evaluation* (pp. 51-61). San Francisco: Jossey-Bass.

Simon, H. A. (1960). *The new science of management decision.* New York: Harper & Row.

Simon, H. A. (1961). *Administrative behavior: A study of decision-making processes in administrative organization* (2nd ed.). New York: Macmillan.

Simon, H. A. (1964). On the concept of organizational goals. *Administrative Science Quarterly, 9,* 1-22.

Sinclair, C., & Frankel, M. (1984). The effect of quality assurance activities on the quality of mental health services. *The Journal of Quality Assurance, 8,* 7-15.

Smith, A., & Cardillo, J. (1979, October). *What does a goal attainment score really measure?* Paper presented at the Evaluation Research Society Annual Meeting, Minneapolis, MN.

Smith, N. L. (1987). Toward the justification of claims in evaluation research. *Evaluation and Program Planning, 10,* 309-314.

Smith, N. L., & Smith, J. K. (1985). State level evaluation uses of cost analysis: A national descriptive survey. In J. S. Catterall (Ed.). *Economic evaluation of public programs* (pp. 83-97). San Francisco: Jossey-Bass.

Sonnichsen, R. C. (1987). Communicating excellence in the FBI. In J. S. Wholey (Ed.), *Organizational excellence: Stimulating quality and communicating value* (pp. 123-141). Lexington, MA: Lexington.

Sonnichsen, R. C. (1988). Advocacy evaluation: A model for internal evaluation offices. *Evaluation and Program Planning, 11* (2), 141-148.

Sonnichsen, R. C. & Schick, G. A. (1986). Evaluation: A tool for management. *FBI Law Enforcement Bulletin, 55* (2), 5-10.

Stelmachers, Z., Lund, S., & Meade, C. (1972). Hennepin County crisis center: Evaluation of its effectiveness. *Evaluation, 1* (1), 61-65.

Thompson, G. E. (1976). *Management science: An introduction to modern quantitative analysis and decision making.* New York: McGraw-Hill.

Thompson, M. S. (1980). *Benefit cost analysis for program evaluation.* Beverly Hills, CA: Sage.

Tripoldi, T., Fellin, P., & Epstein, I. (1971). *Social program evaluation.* Itasca, IL: F. E. Peacock.

Tushman, M. L., & Scanlan, T. J. (1981, June). Boundary spanning individuals: Their role in information transfer and antecedents. *Academy of Management Journal,* 289-305.

Van de Ven, A., & Ferry, D. (1980). *Measuring and assessing organizations.* New York: John Wiley.

Weiss, C. H. (1973, August). *Evaluation in the political context.* Paper presented at the annual meeting of the American Psychological Association, Montreal.

Weist, J. D. & Levy, F. K. (1977). *A management guide to PERT/CPM.* Englewood Cliffs, NJ: Prentice-Hall.

Wholey, J. (1979). *Evaluation: Promise and performance.* Washington, DC: Urban Institute.

Wickstrom, W. (1968). *Managing by and with objectives: Policy 212.* New York: National Industrial Conference Board.

Wildavsky, A. (1972). The self-evaluating organization. *Public Administration Review, 32,* 509-520.

Wildavsky, A. (1975). *Budgeting: A comparative theory of budgeting process.* Boston: Little, Brown.

Winberg, A. R. (1986). A phased approach for conducting program evaluations. *Canadian Journal of Program Evaluation, 1,* 1-11.

Windle, C. (1979). Developmental trends in program evaluation. *Evaluation and Program Planning, 2,* 193-196.

Windle, C., & Neigher, W. (1978). Ethical problems in program evaluation: Advice for trapped evaluators. *Evaluation and Program Planning, 1* (2), 97-107.

Witkin, B. R. (1984). *Assessing needs in social and educational programs.* San Francisco: Jossey-Bass.

Yeaton, W. H., & Redner, R. (1981). Measuring strength and integrity of treatments: rationale, techniques, and examples. In R. F. Conner (Ed.), *Methodological advances in evaluation research.* Beverly Hills, CA: Sage.

Yin, R. K. (1989). *Case study research* (rev. ed.). Beverly Hills, CA: Sage.

Author Index

149

Subject Index

About the Author

Arnold J. Love, Ph.D., is an independent program evaluation consultant based in Toronto, Canada. He holds graduate degrees from the New School for Social Research and the University of Waterloo. He has conducted evaluations and guided the growth of internal evaluation systems in a wide variety of public and community programs, especially in the fields of international development, health, education, and community services.

In addition to his consulting activities, Dr. Love currently teaches program evaluation and information systems design to executive directors and managers of not-for-profit organizations through the Voluntary Sector Management Program of the Faculty of Administrative Studies at York University. He also serves as the manager of the Accreditation Program of the Ontario Association of Children's Mental Health Centres.

Dr. Love's professional work and research reflect his interest in internal evaluation, in developing program evaluation and information management capability in public and community organizations, and in expanding professional development opportunities for evaluators and the users of evaluations. He is an active member of the American Evaluation Association and the Canadian Evaluation Society. He currently serves on the National Council of the Canadian Evaluation Society, the Professional Development Committee of the Society, and on the Council of its Ontario Chapter.

NOTES

NOTES

NOTES

NOTES